PRO ACTIVE
Parenting

JAMES R. LUCAS

HARVEST HOUSE PUBLISHERS
Eugene, Oregon 97402

PROACTIVE PARENTING

Copyright © 1993 by James R. Lucas
Published by Harvest House Publishers
Eugene, Oregon 97402

Library of Congress Cataloging-in-Publication Data
Lucas, J.R. (James Raymond), 1950–
    Proactive parenting / James R. Lucas.
      p. cm.
    ISBN 1-56507-089-5
    1. Parenting—Religious aspects—Christianity. 2. Christian education—Home training. 3. Parenting—Biblical teaching. 4. Family—Religious life. I. Title.
BV4526.2.L823   1993   93-20
248.8'45—dc20   CIP

To Pamela Kay,

my lovely wife and perfect helpmate,
a godly friend and faithful collaborator—
it doesn't get any better than you.
(Proverbs 31:29)

To Laura Christine,

my eldest daughter and wise encourager,
a joyous presence and kindred spirit
who has brought me comfort
from the very first day
that God spoke her into being.
(1 Thessalonians 2:19)

To Peter Barrett,

my eldest son and special friend,
a golden gift to me and a strong leader
in our family for many years to come.
(1 Timothy 4:12)

To David Christopher,

my youngest son and gentle compadre,
an irreplaceable spirit and teacher
of the meaning of love and affection.
(1 Thessalonians 3:9)

To Bethany Gayle,

my youngest daughter and bright light,
a delightful heart and enthusiastic enlivener
of my coming middle age.
(Philippians 1:3)

To Maryl Jan,

my spiritual daughter and covenant friend,
a crystal-clear speaker of truth
and a tender heart
who always encourages me
by her life and love.
(2 John 1)

Contents

Part 3:
Carrying Out the Plan

Your Kids
Are Waiting

Fiction: There's no guarantee that your children will be spiritually strong and prosperous.

Fact: Praise the LORD. Blessed is the man who fears the LORD, who finds great delight in his commands. His children *will be* mighty in the land; the generation of the upright *will be* blessed (Psalm 112:1-2).

Are you trying to raise decent kids?

It just won't be enough.

It won't be enough for you. Having "decent" kids won't be enough to satisfy that deep longing in your heart for each of your children to be special, to make a real difference in this generation—and generations yet unborn.

And it won't be enough for your kids. Being "decent," just staying out of serious trouble, won't be enough to keep them from being affected, or even engulfed, by the evil age in which they live. The spirit of the age speaks too loudly and parades too attractively. Even if your children don't go up in flames, they can be made ineffective in the kingdom of God.

---

*Many parents are beginning to feel that
the whole matter of parenting
is out of their control.*

Your intent as a parent can be good, righteous, true, and pure; but without a clear approach based on the Bible (and precious little else), there's not much of a chance that your children will lead wonderfully special

7

lives. You might even think that what you're currently doing is biblical; but unless it really *is* biblical, I don't think you'll be happy with the result. And neither will God. Dig in deep and meditate on what God is trying to tell you through His Holy Spirit.

We have moved in our day from a sinful age (which all ages are) to an evil age, an age which mocks God and ignores His commands and promises. The bulk of at least two generations has already fallen victim to the spiritual forces in the heavenly realm combined with a rapidly decaying world system that will not honor God.

If the last few generations were to write an epitaph for the ruined lives of their children, it might read:

> Here lie our children.
>
> They asked for bread.
> We gave them treats, and clothes, and houses,
>   and games, and toys, and parties, and
>   movies, and television, and stones.
>
> They asked for fish.
> We gave them schools, and camps, and
>   activities, and music, and dancing, and
>   athletics, and peers, and dates, and snakes.
>
> We gave them everything that money could buy,
>   and we gave them the money, too.
> We gave them everything but an unconquerable
>   spirit and the True Bread of Life.

Unfortunately, many Christians and Christian groups, instead of being the salt of the earth, have either made a pietistic retreat into their homes and churches, or have become virtually indistinguishable from the secular corruption that surrounds them, allowing our culture to disintegrate even further. If unhalted, this will only bring even greater pressure on the family.

Many parents, in fact, are beginning to feel that the whole matter of parenting is out of their control. They seem to have lost control of their children to peers, ungodly celebrities, all forms of media, and the spirit of unbounded independence. Even if they put their children in Christian schools and other Christian activities, they often see their children drawn to the ever-louder beat of the secular drum. Not a few of these children even resent or mock their Christian surroundings. Other children are quieter, but then run away from their parents and their faith when they get away from home. Perhaps this has even happened to you.

And what has been the all-too-frequent response? "Hang on," authors, teachers, and leaders are telling us, "and just try to survive adolescence." This is a "siege" mentality; kind of a "Custer's Last Stand" approach to parenting.

This "reactive" view of parenting will lead to mediocrity or worse, but you don't have to buy into it. You can be a *proactive* parent—one who takes the lead, who gets out in front, who makes good things happen with God's help. You *can* just wait to see what develops—or you can take charge and develop what you want to see.

I don't want you to just *survive* parenting, or end up saying, "Well, we gave it our best shot." I want to elevate your vision of your ministry as a parent. You can't expect to raise extraordinary children unless you first dedicate yourself to parenting, and then learn how to do it.

And this is the key. *You.* Living and growing strong is the primary way of teaching (what Scripture refers to as "discipling") your children to live and grow strong. Although there are methods and techniques to be found in these pages, they are secondary to the major point: If you, the parent, aren't recklessly committed to the Lord, then there's not really very much you can do to raise dedicated, committed children.

Most of all, I don't want you to say, "You know, that book really had some good ideas," and then forget you ever read it. Take your time with this book. Read a section and apply it. Each section is a tool. Get out a pen and mark meaningful ideas. Discuss them with your spouse. Don't feel as though you have to read and apply the whole book at once.

Finally, don't read this book without a Bible in your other hand. Some core Scriptures are written out, but others are given only as references. Be sure to take the time to look them up. Let God speak to your heart.

And here's my hope: That you will actually get off your easy chair and *do* something. Not talk about doing it, or think about doing it, but for our God's sake to actually do it, one principle at a time.

Your kids are waiting.

Part 1

A Call for High Vision

1

A Vision for Parents

Fiction: There's no way to know how your children will turn out.

Fact: Train a child in the way he should go, and when he is old he _will not_ turn from it (Proverbs 22:6).

You can do it.
   That's right. You can really do it. Not you in general, but you specifically. You, the person reading these words, can accomplish what many of the "notables" of our day and of history have failed to accomplish. In the midst of a very evil age, you can parent godly children.
   Wouldn't that be something? Wouldn't you love for people to come up to you and say, "You mean that boy is _your_ son?" Or, "How on earth did you raise _that_ lovely young woman?" Wow! You could put out somebody's eye with the buttons popping off your shirt.
   Don't settle for anything less.
   This is a day in which some very discouraged Christians are beginning to ask some very discouraging questions. But they are really very old questions, asked by God's people in other times and places as cultures began to disintegrate: "Many are asking, 'Who can show us any good?'" (Psalm 4:6). "When the foundations are being destroyed, what can the righteous do?" (Psalm 11:3).

But we who are believers are to rise above the merely natural and find our way with God's help to the *supernatural*. In the first place, apathetic Christianity (what a contradiction in terms!) allowed things to get where they are now. Our whining is not only pathetic, it's misplaced. We are a little like the man who killed his parents, and then threw himself on the mercy of the court because he was an orphan! Several generations of Christians have allowed our culture to die, and now they want the non-Christian world to "give our families a break."

But there will be no break given by this post-Christian culture; no mercy asked, no quarter given. Whatever is recovered for the kingdom of God is going to have to be recovered as it was lost: one value, one principle, one family, one child at a time. *Your* family. *Your* child.

You can do it.

── *Good Christians* ──

Jennifer seemed to be doing so well. She had the highest grades in her class at the Christian school. The teachers all liked her, and the other children usually wanted to spend time with her. She was often given the major role in school plays, and people told her that she looked and dressed "cute." Compared to many of her peers, Jennifer was doing great. Her parents could have sat back and thought they'd done enough.

But Jennifer's heart was full of anger toward God. Her faith and enjoyment of spiritual life were ebbing away. Her resentment of her harsh and angry father colored her life, even as she passed the same treatment along to the younger children in the family. Pride and arrogance, along with an independent spirit, had filled her heart.

Fortunately, Jennifer's mother made the effort to look past the happy veneer and down to Jennifer's deeply troubled heart. Mom refused to be satisfied with the accomplishments or the superficial praise of others. She began to probe Jennifer's thoughts and feelings, to discuss honestly the effect of the father on Jennifer and the family, and to seek pastoral help on ways to both encourage and discipline her daughter.

The result was hope for change on the *inside*, where it really counts.

Given the spiritual assaults on the culture and the family, it *is* the most natural thing in the world to go into a survival mode as a parent. It's easy to feel that as long as you can get your kids through, as long as other people think they're okay, as long as they come out as "good Christians," that's the best you can do. Other "good" Christians will often agree. We can easily persuade ourselves that helping to save our children from the pit and giving them a halfway decent start in life is, in the midst of incredible godlessness, somehow enough.

It is not enough.

It has never been enough—not in any age or place. Jennifer's mother understood. This "plod-through" Christianity has never been sufficient to do the job that God needs to have done. But in this age and place, it's not only not in the ballpark, it's not even near the ticket booth. While the evil age drives many parents and counselors to accept mediocrity as the best they can expect, wise parents will understand that the *evil age itself* is one of the main reasons to raise a truly godly child.

If you were preparing your child to go on a walk through some lush, shady field, you might send him off with a canteen of water and a sandwich. But if you had to prepare your child to walk through a barren, scorching desert, you would certainly send him on his way with all of the provisions for strength that you could think of and that he could carry. You would prepare him for the actual journey that he was to make. Parents, this age is *not* a shady field!

God is clear that He wants powerful, mighty ambas-
sadors to represent His life to the world. All children
have certain gifts and specific abilities in which they can
and must excel for God, and we must surely help them to
develop these areas. But there isn't much to be said for
stopping here and using these kinds of things to show
the world that your children are "good Christians," while
they exhibit little character and make no real impression
on the age. "Adequate" Christianity is not biblical.

Look at history. Look at how much has been accomplished through the efforts of such a very small number
of people. What on earth would happen if every Christian parent would chuck this willingness to be satisfied
with adequacy and choose instead to raise a spiritual
giant of God? A generation of such giants would leave
even *this* sinful world changed dramatically.

If we know Jesus as our personal Savior, we already
have eternal life. We are already in the kingdom of God,
for "our citizenship is in heaven" (Philippians 3:20). We
have a God of power, a Savior of power, a Spirit of power,
and a Word of power. We have a bigger chunk of God's
omniscience available to us in Scripture than many of us
know what to do with. So why are we so lifeless? Why do
we and our children so often act just like everyone else?
Finally and most importantly, why don't we have power?

I'm sure that God knows the answer to these questions. I'm equally sure that He would rather not know—
that He would rather see us living out the power that we
already have in Christ (see 2 Peter 1:3-5).

We *can* be powerful if we choose to be. The Bible says:
"Blessed is the man who fears the LORD, who finds great
delight in his commands" (Psalm 112:1).

We know from Scripture that fear of the Lord defines
a wise man, and that such a man increases in strength,
attacks and destroys the strongholds of the worldly, and
stands immovable against a world that pretends to be
strong but is enslaved by its own weakness. These things

are exquisite in themselves, but Psalm 112 has a series of promises. The first one is this: "His children *will be* mighty in the land; the generation of the upright will be blessed" (verse 2).

What a promise! Please note that it's not a promise that his children will be mighty in heaven (which they, of course, will be), but that they will be mighty *in the land!* Right here and now, you can leave a legacy of power that will continue to change the world long after you've made the voyage to your home country. Your own children may be the very reason, in fact, that society doesn't destroy itself in their lifetime.

How do you get in on this promise? How, you are asking, can I produce mighty children? How can my children have it all? The answer was given before the promise was described. All of God's promises, both for blessing and cursing, are conditional. This wonderful promise is no different.

First, *you* have to fear the Lord. It's quite interesting that the promise is based on *your* fear of the Lord, not on your children's fear of the Lord. The reason is very simple: The best way for your children to learn the fear of the Lord is through being discipled by you as *you* become a God-fearing man or woman (see Nehemiah 7:2).

The second condition for the promise is that you find "great delight in his commands." God has, in a single verse, given both the beginning and ending methods of successful parenting. It starts with the fear of the Lord and ends with finding His commands delightful. He wants you to find them true, and He wants you to obey them in His strength. But this isn't enough. He also wants you to find them delightful—and not just a little delightful, but *greatly* delightful. As John reminds us: "This is love for God: to obey his commands. *And his commands are not burdensome*, for everyone born of God overcomes the world" (1 John 5:3-4). Contrary to so much of the teaching we hear today, God *is* interested in our taking His commands seriously.

What's the bottom line? You as a parent have an ironclad promise that if you think and do certain things, your children will be mighty. Not adequate, not out of trouble, but *mighty*. God has put their outcome partly in your hands. But if you don't take everything that God says and then joyously and immediately put it into practice, God is telling you not to be surprised when your children grow up to be 98-pound spiritual weaklings.

Right here and now, you can leave a legacy that will continue to change the world long after you've made the voyage to your home country.

One of the difficulties you're going to have in raising a child who can truly conquer in this evil age is that you yourself may have grown up in an easier time. Your training might be totally inadequate to deal with what *you* are facing today, much less with what your children are facing. You'll have to let God retrain and restrengthen you before you can do anything for your children. But you must do it, for yourself and them—and you must do it quickly.

It's all too easy to give your children just enough "religion" to inoculate them from the life of power. You can leave them with a life that looks good in a suit, but then wrinkles as the pressure comes. You can manipulate them so that they have too much "religion" to keep them from seeing their weakness and need for God, and too little true religion to allow them to stand.

Only a change in *your* life, only being a man or woman of God, will allow you to be a godly parent and your child, a conqueror. Don't settle for too little. It's easy to do, and you'll hate yourself for it.

Even if your children are "good Christians."
Maybe especially.

__ *The Starting Point* __

Many Christian parents teach their children that the highest gift God has bestowed on them is their personal salvation from the penalty of sin, through the shed blood of the Messiah on the cross. This is certainly the first blessing, the fundamental gift from God upon which all other blessings are based. Without salvation, your children are just wandering prey, lost and bleeding, waiting to be destroyed by the merciless father of lies (see John 8:44).

But is salvation the *highest* possible blessing? Or is the highest blessing justification before God? Could it be the wisdom and power to walk a sanctified life? Or the authority that God has given us on earth? Maybe our deliverance from the full curse of the law (see Deuteronomy 28:15-68; Galatians 3:13)? How about our acceptance by the Lord? Or could it be the good works and related rewards that He has stored up for us? This is a tough question for the simple reason that God has given us so much even though we deserved execution and hell.

But none of these are the *highest* blessing from the hand of God. These are juicy and fabulous, to be sure, but the best is better than all of this. At the point of salvation, God becomes your Abba, your Papa, your Daddy, and you become His child.

It doesn't get any better than that.

How do we know this? "Yet to all who received him, to those who believed in his name, he gave the right to become children of God" (John 1:12). Did you get that? You have a *right* to become God's child, and your children have the same right. God actually uses this awesome blessing to define the magnitude of His love for us (see 1 John 3:1).

There are so many Scripture verses on this subject that it's hard to be selective, but here are a few:

- Ephesians 1:3-8. In love, God planned our adoption. An adopted son in the first century received absolute sonship and had all the rights of a natural son.

- 2 Corinthians 6:16-18. Our adoption is God's plan and His decision. God wasn't forced into adopting us.

- Hebrews 2:11. Jesus agrees with the Father and is not ashamed to call us His brothers!

- Romans 8:15. This adoption has the Spirit of sonship. There's no fear, just love and affection as we cry out, "Papa!"

- Galatians 3:26–4:7. We own the whole estate because our Father owns everything. In fact, it's because He has adopted us as sons that He gives us of His Spirit. We aren't just flesh—we are *spirit of His Spirit*.

God didn't have to offer all of this to us—but praise Him, He did!

If you and your children don't grasp this intimate relationship with God as a loving Father, you and they will never be able to grasp and accept all of the wonderful blessings of God that He wants to shower upon you in this life. These things just won't make sense. Why would God want to listen to me? Why would He care? Why would He rescue me? Why would He want to honor me, for goodness sake?

Because He is your *Papa*.

Your children *can* settle for less. They are His children if they're truly saved, but they can live in such a way as to largely miss enjoying their relationship with their heavenly Father. They can go back to "those weak and miserable principles" (Galatians 4:9) that deny the fatherhood of God—but why on earth would they?

One reason, perhaps the main reason, is that their parents never teach them and show them how to simply rest in the lap of their heavenly Father and "live it up" as a child of the mighty Creator God.

Teach your children often and deeply about their perfect Father; most important of all, let your children see in your walk and life that this God is, without question, their father's Father and mother's Father.

The thing we all want the most from our fathers is love and the commitment that goes along with it. In fact, the first three things we want from our fathers is love, and then love, and finally love, always. *Unfailing* love (see Proverbs 19:22). No backing down, in spite of our mistakes and flaws. God is that kind of father. And He doesn't just want to *treat* you as though He is a Father and have you *act* as though you are His son. He *is* your Father, and you *are* His son!

Teach your children that even if they blow it, even if they make some terrible mistake, God won't cast them out (see John 5:24). He may have to discipline or even punish them severely (see Hebrews 12), but even then His love is the driving force.

Look at the story of the lost son in Luke 15. This is usually used to describe an unsaved person coming to God. But that can't be the only way to look at this story, because the young man is already a son at the beginning of the story, and unsaved people simply aren't children of God. This is, in fact, the ultimate "blown" relationship between a father and his son. Does the father hate the son, look for ways to nail him, hate to see him come back, and give him a crummy place in the pigpen (which is the best that the world had for him)?

No way.

The father sees his son coming back and is filled with compassion. He *runs* to his son, hugs him and kisses him, accepts the repentance even as he cuts his son's speech short, showers him with the best blessings of his house, begins a celebration (with a fattened calf it almost looks as though he's been saving for the occasion), pleads with the older brother to love and forgive (a real lesson for the families and the church), and gives *no hint* that the sonship had ever changed.

It *is* important for us to note that this father didn't go chasing all over to find his son. There does come a time when a father has to let his children reap what they sow and not get in the way of God's discipline. But the point of fatherhood is, if it's real, it can never go away.

After my father and mother separated, I had the privilege of being a "spiritual" father to my younger sister, Patty. When Patty was a teenager and not doing well, we brought her, at my mother's request, to live with my wife Pam and me. (I can still remember Patty telling me at the halfway point of our trip from St. Louis to Kansas City, "Jim, you can take me home now. I see the light, and I'm totally changed!" We kept going.) With God's help, Pam and I had the joy of helping Patty work through many of her problems.

When Patty went back to St. Louis, there was a period of time when she flirted once again with the old "friends" and the old way of life. We just kept praying for her and loving her, but at the same time we knew that she was capable of realizing how empty that way of life was (see Romans 6:21 and 1 Peter 1:18). At that point we recognized that intervention had to come from God, not us.

And after a time, Patty did come back, just like the prodigal son. She gave up the old "friends" and the old habits. She joyfully returned to the family and has since become a responsible and generous person. A few years after her return, I had the privilege and honor of walking her down the aisle as her "spiritual" father (our father had passed away). And not too long ago, she thanked me for loving her when there was no reason left to do it.

Even when we are prodigals, God never stops being the prodigal's Father. He is totally committed, loving, compassionate, forgiving. Somehow, find a way to convey this to your children. And after giving them the truth of the Word of God, there is perhaps no better thing to do than to treat them as God has said He wants to treat you.

___ Son of Nun ___

Once you've gotten hold of the reality of the mighty God of creation being your very own Papa and begin walking in that reality, you will be demonstrating that you are related to the Father "from whom his whole family in heaven and on earth derives its name" (Ephesians 3:15). You'll be taking on the family resemblance, looking more and more like your Father. Ultimately, there's no family except God's family (see Matthew 12:46-50). If you understand this, you're ready to affect history, for one of the joys of Christian parenthood is the prospect that your principles and values and goals can be carried through many generations by your descendants.

Jonathan Edwards is considered to be the most influential American preacher and writer during the Great Awakening of the 1700s. One biographer calls him "one of the greatest philosophers since the days of the apostle Paul and Augustine." His sermon, "Sinners in the Hands of an Angry God," is possibly the most famous and effective message ever delivered on the North American continent.

It is probably no coincidence that his maternal grandfather was the pastor of a church in Northampton, Massachusetts, for more than 50 years, as well as one of the most noted and influential church leaders in all of New England. He personally took young Jonathan under his wings as an apprentice pastor.

Jonathan's father was the pastor of a church in East Windsor, Massachusetts, for 64 years. He was a Latin, Greek, and Hebrew scholar who personally trained his son in language and writing skills. Jonathan's mother was highly respected as an educated woman who loved to read and to encourage her family of 11 children (Jonathan was the only boy!) to be holy and to spend their lives worthily.

The work of these people, going back for generations and invested heavily into one young man, was not wasted. Yours won't be either.

Many parents figure that parenting is an important job, but that it's still peripheral to the real purposes they're supposed to accomplish with their lives. To them, parenting is a job that must be discharged successfully, just like any other effort they might undertake. They try to prepare their children to lead their own lives, and believe that their children will then work to achieve their own goals, on a separate path.

Friends, parenting isn't just another job on the long list of jobs that you've been assigned; not simply a good work to finish and then set aside. This is how you will be remembered in the real world for *generations*. This is a way to affect countless people to at least the third and fourth generations. And not *just* your descendants, but all people who come into *contact* with your descendants!

There are, of course, many obvious scriptural examples. Abraham believes God and the promise is carried through Isaac and Jacob and beyond in a very clear and interconnected fashion. David, a man of wisdom who conceives the temple, raises Solomon, a wiser man who actually builds the temple. Timothy is encouraged by Paul to remember the sincere faith "which first lived in your grandmother Lois and in your mother Eunice" (2 Timothy 1:5). This principle works with the wicked as well, as can be seen by reading about the later kings of God's people. With few exceptions, each one is worse than any who preceded him, but his behavior is always compared to and connected with that of his rotten ancestors.

Scripture also tells us, "A good name is more desirable than great riches; to be esteemed is better than silver or gold" (Proverbs 22:1). This doesn't just mean your reputation; without doubt, this also includes your name and the images and ideas your name will raise. This is clearly a heritage that will be passed on to your children and is immeasurably more important than any material trinkets that you might leave to them.

If you have any doubt that your good (or bad) name will be preserved through your children, why do you think Scripture says that the father of a wise man can answer anyone who treats him with contempt (see Proverbs 27:11)? Or that there is no joy for the father of a fool (see Proverbs 17:21)? Or that anyone who would lead God's people must be judged on the basis of his children's lives and behavior as well as his own (see 1 Timothy 3:4-5 and Titus 1:6)?

And a good name is not something that just happens, like winning a door prize. Scripture says: "Let love and faithfulness never leave you; bind them around your neck, write them on the tablet of your heart. *Then* you will win favor and a good name in the sight of God and man" (Proverbs 3:3-4).

So it's pretty clear that the value of your name is in your own hands, as you walk a life of love and faithfulness—or a life of leaking values and wastefulness. How this is passed on to your children is also in your hands, even after they've become adults. And how you will be remembered is up to you.

One of my favorite examples of the efforts of a man of God living with power through his child is the scriptural example of Joshua son of Nun. Now, we have absolutely no account of the life of this father called Nun. The only thing we know is that he is the son of Elishama and the father of Joshua. Most of the people listed in chronologies in Scripture are never again discussed, and if they are not discussed, their names are usually dropped. But here we have this person named Nun, who is himself not discussed, but whose name appears more than 25 times.

And how does it appear? Always in conjunction with the name of his son, Joshua. Joshua is constantly referred to as "Joshua son of Nun." This can't be just for clarification of which Joshua we are talking about; it's not like there are a bunch of Joshuas leading the people into the Promised Land. If this were so, it would be akin to the media's habit of referring to President Truman as "Harry S. Truman," to distinguish him from all of the other presidents named Harry Truman.

Where do you think Joshua came from? He was a powerful man of God, and one who must have been raised by another powerful man of God. God, I think, really believes in this business of blessing and cursing families. The story of Joshua shows the blessing that must have come to him, in part, through the faithfulness of his father. God honored the parent for the outstanding faith and values that were so evident in his son. He reminds us of the son's starting point—a godly parent.

So please—for our God's sake, for your sake, and for the sake of countless people yet unborn—do an excellent job of raising little Harold or Irene.

Son—or daughter—of *you*.

___ *The Upside-Down Kingdom* ___

"There is a way that seems right to a man, but in the end it leads to death" (Proverbs 14:12).

What does it mean when it says that there is a way that "seems" right? Well, in every field of human endeavor, including parenting, there are two basic approaches: God's way and man's way. There are always two paths, two roads, even for the Christian.

But this verse tells us even more than that. It tells us that there is a way, a direction, that's going to sound good. You're going to hear about it or read about it, and it's going to click with your human nature.

And that's the problem. It clicks. It *seems* right. But it *isn't* right. It doesn't work, because you get the opposite results of what you had hoped for (see Acts 27:9-14). Few men would plan a way that would lead to death, but that's just what this road that seems so right leads to—death. You may not have ever applied this Scripture to parenting, but it applies directly and absolutely.

Our culture is chock-full of ideas on parenting. Many are very bad, some are weird, and a few are beyond incredible. Perhaps the worst of the lot is the idea that you as a parent don't have the right to "impose" your values on your child (more on this in Chapter 4). When some people start telling us about the reasons behind this—the dignity of each child, the faultiness in our own character—it can start to sound logical, even right. But what's the end of it? You don't impose your values. The enemy imposes his. Your children die—spiritually, mentally, emotionally, even physically. You lose.

On the other hand, many of God's ideas—also called "truth"—sound strange. They just don't click. It's almost as though He planned life in such a way that the things that seem good aren't and the things that sound strange are wonderful; as if He turned things upside down.

"Do not deceive yourselves. If any one of you thinks he is wise by the standards of this age, he should become a 'fool' so that he may become wise. For the wisdom of this world is foolishness in God's sight" (1 Corinthians 3:18-19). Occasionally, the godless hit upon a truth (see Proverbs 14:33), but if you're listening to the Dr. Spocks and their followers on a regular basis, you're in big trouble.

We need to train ourselves to listen closely to the things that sound strange, the upside down truths that define the kingdom of God. And then we need to turn our children's lives upside down with the power of this "foolishness"—that just happens to be absolute truth.

What are some of these truths?

- If you try to save your own life, you will lose it; if you "lose" your life to Christ you will save it. To put it another way, God always gives His best to those who leave the choice with Him. Does this have application to where and how you spend your time?

• If you exalt or promote yourself and your interests, you'll be humbled or even torn down; if you humble yourself, God will exalt you at just the right time. Does this have application to jockeying for position at work or church? Do your children hear you speak about humble service to your employer and church family?

• If you hoard your possessions for yourself, you'll lose them all; if you generously share with others, you will gain more and more. Does this have application to your family finances and how much (and how willingly) you give back to God? Do your children see you giving up personal pleasures for the benefit of others?

• If you try to live a good life in your own strength, you'll be wiped out; if you acknowledge your own weakness, God's strength will be made perfect in you. Does this have application to how your children see you coping (or not coping) with stress?

When you hear an idea in the Word of God that sounds upside-down, think about it hard. Maybe *you're* the one who's upside-down.

— *Our Life's Work* —

We all remember the old saying, "God helps those who help themselves." It's an interesting thought that sums up an entire religious philosophy. It implies that it is our job as Christians to try to live for the Lord, and the Lord's job to bless us in these righteous efforts. It says that "the Lord provides the fish, but we have to dig up the bait" and simply, that we had better work very hard if we expect to get any blessings. There's only one problem with this neat little idea.

It is totally wrong.

God is *not* obligated to help those who help themselves, and you shouldn't teach your children so. God doesn't even enjoy helping those who help themselves, as evidenced by Scripture:

- Trying to worship God in your own strength doesn't work (Exodus 32:21-35).

- Trying to clear up sin in your own strength doesn't work (Numbers 14:26-45).

- Trying to fight spiritual battles in your own strength doesn't work (Judges 7:2).

- Trying to obey God's Word in your own strength doesn't work (1 Samuel 15:10-23).

- Trying to get God's blessing in your own strength doesn't work (2 Chronicles 16:9-13).

God wants His people to rely on Him, and Him alone, for strength and power. He wants them to cease from self and the efforts of self. Good actions not prompted by faith and strengthened by the Lord miss the mark. It's true that I can do all things; but only because I have the full power of God at my disposal. I *can* do all things— through my Lord who strengthens my spirit.

Teach your children this truth. Don't let them get out on their own without a good, solid sense of their own helplessness and inadequacy. If they don't have this, their pride, along with Satan and the world system, will tear them down to a level from which they might never recover. They need to know that without God they are nothing, can do nothing, can become nothing, can have nothing. Hammer this home consistently with your children, and teach them that those who help themselves have a fool for an assistant.

This truth—our absolute dependence upon the Lord for true success—should even color our bragging about our kids. The only time we should really brag is if and when our children step out from the ordinary and do something because they are sensitive to the invisible realm—like doing something around the house without being asked.

And as soon as we brag about it, we should pray for our children on that very point. Satan can't read our minds but he can hear our words. Nothing could delight him more than to tear your children down at the very point of success, by causing them to fall or by turning it into a point of pride.

Even better than this kind of bragging is to teach your children (and yourself) to boast about and delight in weaknesses just as Paul did. The great result of this kind of bragging is that Christ's power will rest on you (see 2 Corinthians 12:9-10). A believer who boasts about his helplessness is a Christian to be reckoned with.

Teach your children that absolutely *nothing* is impossible with our God, and that absolutely *everything* is possible to the person—child or otherwise—who believes (see Psalm 34:8-10).

If you must teach the "old saying," at least teach it accurately. God *does* help those who help themselves—to Him.

If you will grasp the vision laid out in this chapter and the rest of this book, and apply it with your own children, you can achieve great victory for God. No enemy, no corruption, nothing will be able to keep you from parenting a godly child. You can do it.

You *must* do it.

Your great-grandchildren will thank you.

2

The Importance of High Expectations

Fiction: You shouldn't expect too much from your children.

Fact: Aim for perfection (2 Corinthians 13:11).

*"Aim for **what**? Perfection?* You must be kidding."

No, I'm not.

More important than that, *God* isn't kidding. He wants you to set your sights high, to the top of a lofty mountain. Our Father actually wants us to aim for perfection. We serve a God who says, without hesitation or qualification, "Be holy, because I am holy" (Leviticus 11:44-45; 19:2; 1 Peter 1:16). In 1 Peter it says right before that, "But just as he who called you is holy, so be holy in *all* you do" (verse 15).

God is very serious about the fact that He wants you to aim for perfection. Is it possible that He doesn't include parenting in this? Or that He doesn't really care whether or not you teach your children to aim for perfection? How can we settle for so little, when our Father offers—and requires—so much?

Too many parents in our day have been browbeaten and discouraged into believing that they cannot or should not set high standards for themselves and their children. They're told that it isn't "fair" to expect too much. But, folks, there's one thing that's true about everything in life: You'll never get more than what you aim for.

When I was in high school, I practiced shooting on a large rifle range. I was told that if I wanted to have the highest possible score, I had to hit the center of the target. I knew, without being told, that in order to hit the center I had to *aim* for the center.

Brilliant.

And yet many so-called experts on parenting don't even latch on to something this fundamental. If you want the highest possible score ("Well done, good and faithful servant" [Matthew 25:23]), you have to hit the center ("The father of a righteous man has great joy" [Proverbs 23:24]). And if you want to hit this center, you have to aim for it.

I didn't always hit the center, of course. There were times when I was glad I wasn't hitting innocent by-standers. But if I hadn't been aiming for the center of the target, there's no telling *what* I would have hit.

As a parent, you can aim for perfection: in yourself, your parenting skills, and your children. You *must* aim for perfection. You might make a mistake and get less, but you'll never get more than what you aim for. Aiming for perfection as a parent is not only acceptable—it's *crucial* if you want to raise a godly child.

But before we discuss how you can develop high expectations and put them into practice, let's look at some modern "wisdom" that can shred your vision to pieces.

__ *Emperors Without Clothes* __

It's time that someone said it: The emperor has no clothes.

William Kirk Kilpatrick has said it in several books discussing the attempted mixture of Christianity and psychology, the so-called study of the mind. But few people seem to be listening, compared to the thousands or millions who wait for the stale crumbs that slide off the tilting table of modern psychology.

The real question is: When are you going to turn off your radio and television and stop *listening* to this rubbish? When are you going to "turn away from godless chatter and the opposing ideas of what is falsely called knowledge, which some have professed *and in so doing have wandered from the faith*" (1 Timothy 6:20-21)?

There is a fundamental difference between the Bible and psychology: The Bible focuses on God and uses God's words to describe life; psychology focuses on self and creates its own vocabulary to make its teachings sound modern and scientific and worthwhile, when they are very often none of those things.

Consider how psychology divides a person up into stages. God calls people infants, children, men or women, and also by their family positions—son, daughter, father, mother. And the psychologists? They have toddlers and "terrible twos" and pubescents and adolescents and teenagers and on and on. Then these various groups get afflicted with hormonal attacks and premenstrual syndrome and menopause and mid-life crisis, and if they're not careful, with manic depression and paranoia and schizophrenia. I mean, we're talking *science* here, right?

Wrong.

Parents of "adolescents" have been told that the one thing that dominates their children's lives more than anything else in their transition from child to adult is their hormones. But what does the Word of God say?

> But I see another law at work in the members of my body, waging war against the law of my mind and making me a prisoner of the law of sin at work within my members. What a wretched man I am! Who will rescue me from this body of death? Thanks be to God—through Jesus Christ our Lord! (Romans 7:23-25).

God calls it "the law of sin." The psychologists call it "hormones." Once you've fallen for the idea that your child is totally driven by physical forces outside of his or her or your control, you and your child are absolved of any real responsibility. And so the "logical" advice given to parents of adolescents becomes: "Get them through it."

Some vision, isn't it? Is simple survival the ringing call to victory given in Romans 8? God talks about saving us and sanctifying us and working His victorious Son's life through us every minute of our lives. There's no "getting through it" anywhere in the Bible. But there is a lot about giving in to the flesh on one hand, and a lot about conquering sin through the power of God on the other.

And then where do the psychologists take us? Since your child can't control himself, they say it's useless to set high standards. In spite of the Bible's call to aim for perfection, we are told to lower our standards so our children won't become frustrated. Try to find a biblical basis for *that* teaching. You can search for the rest of your life, and you'll never see God willing to lower His standards.

God does say that we shouldn't "exasperate" our children (Ephesians 6:4). But He goes on to say *"instead*, bring them up in the training and instruction of the Lord."* Do you see what this is saying? We exasperate our children when we *don't* set standards high, when we *don't* ground them, in spirit and in practice, "in the training and instruction of the Lord."

Donald Barr, quoted in *World* (May 19, 1986), said:

> Adolescence appears to be a relatively modern invention, and the romantic wretchedness of it appears to be more modern still; and it could be argued that many of those wretched, stewing identity crises occur precisely because adolescents seek

to build their identities as adolescents instead of reaching out confidently for adult identities.

Amen.

Don't listen to people who focus attention on self and flesh and use terms different from God's to get us, even unintentionally, to think about life differently from God. Don't listen, no matter how decent their motives. Don't listen, because what they're selling is a lie.

___ *Dare to Be Different* ___

If you're at all like me, you don't remember very much about your childhood. One thought, however, has not escaped me since my eighth-grade teacher spent so much time pounding it into my head. She had a motto for life, and she intended that we adopt it as our motto as well: Dare to be different.

This statement says so much. Most of us know in our hearts that we're supposed to be different, that God made us to be unique, that we have a special life to lead and a special contribution to make. But somehow this idea becomes so fuzzy and dim over time, that even reading about it brings only a faint sense of longing and a sorrowful sense that you've missed something very important.

Now, I am not talking about being different for the sake of being different; this approach belongs to the fanatic or fool. I am talking about being different for the sake of Christ. What I mean is the living of a different kind of life, a different quality of life, a wonderfully noteworthy life—a life that leaves a deep mark on a granite-hard world.

Many people are bored with their own lives. Given the inexpressibly wondrous gift of life, they waste it by just "putting in time." Days blend into other days, weeks into months, months into years—and all the while no mark is left, no special loves are grown, no joyous victories are won. Another year spent, just like the last one. Others chase the "American Dream" of a good education, which gets you a good job, which gets you a lot of money and debt, which gets you a house and a car and two televisions, which gets you . . . nothing.

God didn't make you or your children for such a tasteless existence.

There are unlimited ways to be different for Christ. Some of these ways may be knocking at your door right now. Stop, listen, and write them down. Then do them.

But being different has a cost, and your children need to understand this very early and very clearly. If you've taught them to "continue in what [they] have learned and have become convinced of" (2 Timothy 3:14), then you must also teach them that "everyone who wants to live a godly life in Christ Jesus will be persecuted" (2 Timothy 3:12). This doesn't just mean physical torture or imprisonment; in our society, at least at the moment, this is not the most likely possibility. For now, their persecution will more often come in the form of ridicule, rejection, and hatred.

How can you and your children be different? Try speaking the truth, in love but without compromise, to your family and friends. Do something nice for someone because they *haven't* asked you to. Turn off the television and read the Word of God for four hours tonight instead. Proclaim the Word of God at school or at work or in your neighborhood, and do it without embarrassment. Make a picket sign and protest abortion, or pornography, or the fact that they won't let your God into their "public" schools.

There are unlimited ways to be different for Christ. Some of these ways may be knocking at your door right now. Stop, listen, and write them down. Then do them. By your example and exhortation, you'll be able to teach your child not only to *be* different for Christ, but also to *value* being different and to rejoice in any suffering or rejection that might come as a result.

But first, you must *teach* your children the meaning of this "dare to be different" business. Look with them at the life of Jesus or Paul; these men were so different and so daring, they startled their world as they drew the line of decision down its middle. Teach them about risk and courage—and that God's wisdom and power are behind it all, making the apparent human risk seem insignificant by comparison. And, of course, you must teach them about the good kinds of "different" and the rebellious, evil varieties; the difference between Jesus' revolution of truth and love and man's revolution *against* truth and love.

Teach your children the words of Robert Ingersoll: "It is a blessed thing that in every age someone has had the individuality enough and courage enough to stand by his own convictions."

Then teach them to *dare* to be different. Daring includes actions as well as thoughts and words. Talk is truly cheap; teach them to do, as they do it with you.

I have challenged my son Peter to be different by controlling what he looks at or allows himself to see. I have told him that there is no point of the devil's attack that has more potential for the destruction of a man's spirit (see 1 Corinthians 6:18-20). Any man who denies this is fooling himself or trying to fool you.

I have dared to be different in this area as well. I expect Peter not to watch inappropriate television programs or movies (or commercials!), and I don't either. We throw sections of the newspaper away without looking at them. We leave the public pool if an immodestly dressed woman shows up. Yes, it's inconvenient, and yes, it can shorten a time of family fun. But we don't care. We've chosen to be different.

Recently I was made aware that Peter is now making this choice for himself. As a family we went to a major art fair with his art teacher. The teacher later told me that whenever Peter came up to something "not good," he would walk a big circle way around it—whether I was nearby or not. Another time, Peter told his mom and me after the fact that he had chosen not to accept an invitation to a party because he suspected some "marginal" movies might be shown.

Peter has chosen to be different, and he *is* different— in one of the most critical areas of a man's life. He has given himself the opportunity to think and act rightly, and to have pure and solid friendships with women throughout his life. Some men take dares by doing something death-defying, to show they are "men." Peter has taken the dare to do something *truly* manly, to show that he is death-defying.

None of your teaching or instruction will mean anything if they don't see you doing something. Nothing discussed here will work unless you dare to be different yourself. It's just too unlikely that your children will dare to be or do *anything* if you won't.

Dare to be different. There's nothing like it.

___ *Expectant Parents* ___

How old should your child be before you begin to challenge him to deal in a godly and creative way with the issues facing him in the world in which he lives? While we're at it, how old should *you* be before you start doing these things?

If you're old enough to read, you're old enough. In fact, you're several years past old enough. You should be finding yourself challenged by the Holy Spirit daily and into the Word frequently enough that you're finding godly and creative answers to the problems and opportunities that find their way into your life.

One of those opportunities is the child—already conceived and shampooing himself with tuna fish, or a still-hoped-for blessing from God—that prompted you to pick up this book. And this new person should also be challenged to use the prompting of the Spirit and the guidance of the Word to find godly and creative answers for his life.

How do you do that? In your own spirit you should start questioning things early, keep at it relentlessly with God's strength, and finish strong. You need the determination of the tortoise more than the speed of the hare to aid you in your search for the truth; a powerful life in the Lord is built up daily, in the little things of life as well as the spectacular. Your children need you to run your race well. By watching you, they'll learn how and why to run, in what direction, for how long, and what to do if they fall down.

After you begin running a good race, challenge your children to run the kind of race that you're running.

You don't have the right to challenge them to run any harder.

___ *The Joneses* ___

At any time, one of the easiest things for a parent to do is to compare his children with each other or with other people's kids. Satan would love for you to do this because it harms your goal of parenting holy children.

As you begin to challenge your children, even at a young age, to be decently different and to choose wisdom over knowledge or popularity, you may be tempted to make comparisons with other families. These comparisons can be either positive ("our son isn't as godly as their son") or negative ("no one else's children are godly, so I guess we can't expect too much"). Don't make comparisons! According to Scripture, if you do this you are *not wise* (see 2 Corinthians 10:12).

When I speak of the importance of high expectations, I am not talking about a competition among Christians. I am talking about a competition that each Christian participates in alone: the running of his own race in order to get the prize (see 1 Corinthians 9:24-27). The higher the prize sought, the more strict the training required to win it. It doesn't matter if the runner beats everyone else if he or she doesn't "run in such a way as to get the prize."

And it's not a race of knowledge and credentials; it's a race of godly wisdom and character. God's wisdom isn't a matter of what you know, although knowing true things about life is very important. It's a matter of what you're *like*: "Who is wise and understanding among you? Let him show it by his good life, by deeds done in the humility that comes from wisdom" (James 3:13).

Nothing is more plentiful in some churches today than children who have lots of Bible knowledge and "God words," and little or no character. There simply aren't any "deeds done in the humility that comes from wisdom." If you fall for the veneer of knowledge and wholesomeness, and don't look for character, you're a foolish parent who deserves the foolish children who will bring you grief.

God's wisdom is "first of all pure; then peace-loving, considerate, submissive, full of mercy and good fruit, impartial and sincere" (James 3:17). Truly wise people don't try to amaze other believers with exhibitions of knowledge.

Comparisons with others on the downward side can also be devastating. If you expect only what you see in the majority of families around you, you're in for a big disappointment. Most families today are *drowning*. They don't have any answers, and they don't even know where to look for them. To settle for the norm today is to settle for "getting by."

So pray for the Joneses.

But don't try to keep up with them.

___ *Truth and Consequences* ___

Your mission is to build godly wisdom and character into your children. It's absolutely crucial that you help them see the stunning victory that awaits a life of faith, and the smashing defeat that awaits the life of self.

"Truth or Consequences" was a popular old television game show. We must not have watched too closely, however, because we don't seem to understand the consequences of missing the truth. And we also don't understand the consequences, the value, of having a clear picture of the truth. It's costing us, and our descendants, a free and peaceful future.

We live in a day when there are so many horrible consequences to so many horrible ideas that the truth doesn't even seem to be an important factor anymore. We read and watch and believe almost totally worthless newspapers, magazines, radio and television programs, and "authoritative" studies every day while our Bibles collect dust. Folks, this stuff isn't wrong because it's secular or humanistic or any other fancy philosophy; it's wrong because it's *wrong*.

"Now," you might be saying, "that sounds pretty simplistic to me." We'd better *get* pretty simplistic fast. The lying juggernaut is trying to roll over you and your children right now, and only a clear and simple understanding of the truth is going to keep it from succeeding. Paul said, "For we are not unaware of [Satan's] schemes" (2 Corinthians 2:11); but the way most Christians are acting, it would be more accurate to say that we are unaware of both Satan *and* his schemes.

You must first learn—and then teach your children to recognize—the underlying principle in each situation that you and they encounter. You can't solve the problem—you can't even *understand* the problem—unless you're looking at it from God's perspective. And then you want to look for God's solution, outlined in His Word and in your heart, and begin to apply it in your family and church.

For example, we have made it a habit in our family to take a close look together at marriages with which at least one of us is familiar. We discuss a marriage in light of God's definition of marriage. We do this with our two older children, but often the younger two are listening in because we know some of what is said is going to be absorbed. We encourage the children to make their own observations.

We recently talked about Randy and Cathy's marriage. This couple was obviously offering each other little but animosity. We explored the needs and brokenness that both of them brought to the marriage, and the myth they believed that marriage would solve all of their problems and make them "happy."

We also discussed Bob and Joanne's marriage. Bob's lack of communication and tenderness had produced a cold, hard response from Joanne. We discussed how their relationship was more of a sharing of duties than a real marriage.

The purpose of these discussions is to let our children see clearly what produces bad marriages and what produces good ones. We're helping them develop a set of criteria to use if and when their "big moment" of decision arrives. You have to be careful not to gossip about others, to be sure. But you *have* to dissect life together, if you don't want your children to be a bad example used by some other parents around a dinner table in 10 or 20 years.

Get yourself and your children back into the basics of God's truth, so that together you'll be able to see the fundamental absolutes and principles that are *really* governing life and causing the consequences that we see and experience. Don't rely on your own common sense or on the world's common foolishness. Keep the lies out of your thinking, even the small lies, for as Paul said, "a little yeast works through the whole batch of dough" (1 Corinthians 5:6).

We and our children must deny the principles of this evil age and focus all of our attention on the true principles of the Word of God. If we do, the positive consequences will reverberate through generation after generation and will bless countless people for decades to come.

Quintessence: Is He the Best, __ or Isn't He? __

As soon as we begin to set our sights on the glorious goal of parenting a child of godly character and, in so doing, begin to understand the critical need for high expectations, an important question begins to crowd into our minds: Can he really be the very best that God intended him to be?

Yes, he can. Your child can be the quintessential Christian champion. And here's more. You can be, too.

What on earth is that? *Quintessence* is "the essence of a thing in its most concentrated form. . . . The most typical example; the consummate instance of a quality." People should be able to look at each one of us and our children and say, "So *that's* a Christian!" Christ fully reflected the Father. We are supposed to fully reflect Christ. If Jesus was a man of outstanding character and we are supposed to walk as Jesus did, how can we settle for anything less?

Some may think I'm talking about lifting ourselves up, about things that could lead to pride. Nothing could be further from the truth. I'm talking about living a life that embodies Christian character in its most concentrated form; a life that makes people sit up and take notice—of our Father and our family and the principles that undergird our lives.

In fact, we aren't being honest if we won't admit that we want our children to be one of the best at what they are and do. We want them to have a tremendous impact on their world. In fact, this desire is more than natural for the godly Christian; it's *super*natural. God desires godly offspring, and we, because we are made in His image, desire the same thing. Pride could get in here, but there's a desire that's right, a hope for children who "shine like stars in the universe" (Philippians 2:15).

Paul goes on to say that he wants his readers to be this kind of believer so that he can "boast on the day of Christ that [he] did not run or labor for nothing" (verse 16). Paul didn't boast about himself, but he *did* boast about the fruits of his labors, about the Christians who were "without fault" (verse 15). We have got to get past this false humility that denies some basic scriptural truths: We're in a race to win the prize, and the reward comes as a result of our work in Christ's strength for others.

Listen to Paul: "For what is our hope, our joy, or the crown in which we will glory in the presence of our Lord Jesus when he comes? Is it not you? Indeed, you are our glory and joy" (1 Thessalonians 2:19-20). And how much more so of our own flesh and blood! We should want our children to be the very best they can be and look forward to the day when we can glory in them in the very presence of the Lord Jesus. What an exciting thought!

This joy of glorying in the success of another was brought home to me by my sister Patty when she was a little girl and I had gone off to college. I didn't think about her relating to what I was doing at all, until one day I received a note from her. "I told my friends that my big brother went to college," she wrote, "and I was acting big about you to them." Some of her feelings might have been childish, of course, but the idea was pretty basic: This person belongs to me—and isn't he special!

Often, though, when we tell ourselves and others that we want children who'll reach the pinnacle of Christian joy, peace, satisfaction, wisdom, and power, we start focusing on things. We think of picking the right schools, the right friends, the right career or vocation, the right marriage partner, the right church. Of course these things are important, even crucial; but our children will never reach the epitome of excellence unless we give them the one thing that is guaranteed to bring them honor in all of these areas for the rest of their lives. You must work to give your child a lowly spirit.

What? A lowly spirit? Am I kidding? No, I'm not kidding. More importantly, God isn't kidding. He says, "A man's pride brings him low, but a man of lowly spirit gains honor" (Proverbs 29:23). The way to honor—so much deeper and longer lasting than fame—is to cultivate and cherish a lowly spirit.

One of the reasons this can sound like such a strange idea is that we parents don't even know what a lowly spirit is. We can, perhaps, almost picture Jesus as a person of lowly spirit, but we have a hard time escaping the idea that that was His *job*. Being lowly was part of being the Savior, and now that's done and we can all get on with our lives.

But God says we are all to be like Jesus, which means, among other things, to be lowly in spirit.

There are two things that a lowly spirit is not. The first is that a lowly spirit isn't proud. The way you work on this with your children is to let them know that pride is disgusting to God and disgusting to you (see Luke 16:15). You need to make them understand that pride in word or action will not be tolerated by God or by you. Listen and watch closely for any signs of pride, and when they come up, move into action.

But being without overt pride isn't necessarily the same as being lowly in spirit. We can pound overt pride out of their lives, but leave the pride itself within, waiting to come out in self-glorification later. We need to give our children a full understanding of what it means to "have the mind of Christ" (1 Corinthians 2:16). We need them to realize how great God is, how small they are, and how much God will bless them and use them if they will only get themselves out of the way. We need to convince them to move only in the light of His presence.

Secondly, a lowly spirit isn't a *beaten* spirit. We want to work the pride out while we work godly humility and gentleness in. We never want to beat the pride out while we work only worthlessness and bitterness in. There are already too many beaten Christians and way too many proud Christians. Neither is going to be blessed, and neither is going to gain honor.

So how do we learn to have a lowly spirit? Many Christians have lived a long time without one, and hidden pride can be so very hard to detect. Here are some suggestions: First, have a quiet time with your Lord and ask Him to help you; second, have a quiet time with your spouse and ask him to help you; and third, have a quiet time with your spiritual shepherd and ask him or her to help you. The part of you that doesn't want to do these things is the pride part.

One final thought: Let your children be the godliest "them" they can possibly be, not the godliest "you" that they can possibly mimic. Let them use you as an example of a developing lowly spirit, but even in that, let *you* only be an arrow pointing toward the Master.

Is your child the best, or isn't he? That's really the wrong question.

The right question is: Is he lowly enough in spirit to be called great by Almighty God (see Isaiah 66:2)?

___ Crowns of Splendor ___

We all give our children gifts, but we should note this: A child can't receive anything greater than wisdom. It's a simple fact and one which should lead us to make their getting of wisdom a major priority. You should want nothing less than a little Solomon.

Now, you can't *make* a child be wise. Children's hearts must deal with or avoid God directly; the ultimate responsibility for this is out of your hands. You aren't a mediator between God and your children, because Christ already has that job. All you can do is make the choice for them as simple as possible, so that each one of them can say with Solomon: "When I was a boy in my father's house . . . he taught me and said, 'Lay hold of my words with all your heart. . . . Wisdom is supreme; therefore get wisdom. Though it cost all you have, get understanding'" (Proverbs 4:3-7).

The cost of getting wisdom, to you as a parent, is your time. You must talk and live these words *constantly*, so that your children will accept this manner of life as *normal*. They must be immersed in wisdom, so that their manner of thinking and speaking flows in these deep channels. In short, they must stop speaking English and start speaking wisdom.

Obviously they'll have a hard time speaking wisdom with you if wisdom is only in *your* heart and head and not in theirs. This special language has to be part of their nature, too. But you must understand that it'll take them time to learn it, and Satan will oppose their education in every possible way. This evil creature who speaks only in lies hates wisdom—not the least reason being that he will never again understand your child once this little one begins speaking it.

The process of learning wisdom must certainly start with learning the words. The vocabulary of wisdom is Scripture, and every child should be encouraged to read or listen to massive chunks of it. They should be taught to memorize, but only passages that have special meaning to or for them. And it's crucial that you get this wisdom into their heads when they're *little*.

The book of Proverbs is especially useful for promoting this wisdom. We have established wisdom charts in our home to encourage this. These can be homemade or store-bought monthly calendars that contain a verse or two of Scripture, some personal thoughts of the child, and some interesting art work. Each day of wisdom reading or listening earns a sticker; a whole month earns dinner out for the family (which gives all of us incentive for the child to get wisdom) or some other tangible reward. These charts are posted in the kitchen and explained to any visitors, preferably within earshot of the child.

It's important, even for little children, to meditate on God's Word in private. I recorded Proverbs for our children and explained the verses as I went. My wife recorded the Psalms. Whether you buy tapes or record your own, it's really exciting to see a little one huddled up next to his tape recorder, soaking up God's Word.

And more is needed. This wisdom must be related to the child's world—to school, peers, world events, sorrows, joys, or anything that's covered by their wisdom vocabulary. They must see how wisdom works and how foolishness works. They must learn to differentiate between short-term and long-term effects and to know that ultimately, wisdom is rewarded and foolishness brings on its own built-in destruction.

Still more is needed. True wisdom goes beyond the head and into the heart, and starts with a holy fear of the Lord God Almighty. Too many of us miss teaching this. We talk a lot about God's love and don't stress the importance, the *practical* importance, of His justice. We have to give our children an honest, realistic, down-to-earth appreciation of the fact that they're in the constant and unavoidable presence of a God who will judge them with perfect and inarguable justice.

It's too easy for us to teach our children about a soft, puny, Milquetoast God who really isn't paying close attention to what's going on down here. A God who loves us "just the way we are," even if the way we are is spitting in His face and bringing disgrace to His name. The real God isn't like that. A little reverent awe around your house is a must. A lot of it will produce children in whom the Lord delights (see Psalm 147:11). Scripture tells us that true and godly wisdom begins with this basic attitude toward God.

This respect and reverence makes way for a deep and genuine love of God. Only when your child appreciates what God expects and what God hates can he really begin to appreciate God for not pouring out heavenly wrath and displeasure right on his head. Jesus reminded us that he who is forgiven of much will be more grateful and loving than he who is forgiven of little (see Luke 7:47).

The child who understands God's close monitoring and pure standards will have a much better chance of knowing how much he's been forgiven. He'll know that "to fear the LORD is to hate evil" (Proverbs 8:13); and he'll have the valuable possession of the truth that "the fear of the LORD is a fountain of life, turning a man from the snares of death" (Proverbs 14:27). With this understanding, your child can truly love God with a devotion that involves his whole being. The payoff is a big one: "Esteem her [wisdom], and she will exalt you; embrace her, and she will honor you. She will set a garland of grace on your head and present you with a crown of splendor" (Proverbs 4:8-9).

I don't know exactly what this crown is, but it sounds mighty fine.

I've got an order in for four.

3

Excellent Communication: Crawl Inside a Heart

Fiction: It's the generation gap. Parents can't understand kids, and kids won't understand parents!

Fact: These commandments that I give you today are to be upon your hearts. Impress them on your children (Deuteronomy 6:6-7a).

You've got to crawl inside your children's hearts. And it can be a very challenging journey.

In the first place, God reminds us how deep and potentially impenetrable a heart can be: "Each heart knows its own bitterness, and no one else can share its joy" (Proverbs 14:10). Without a balance, this could be pretty discouraging. But God also says, "Rejoice with those who rejoice; mourn with those who mourn" (Romans 12:15).

Secondly, it's too easy to miss the golden opportunities our children present. My own father had much to share with his five children, but he couldn't because he worked two jobs, seven days a week. Too many fathers and mothers are just not there most of the time.

In the third place, the time you do have together can be swallowed up by activities and idle chitchat about the miscellaneous details of everyday life. Now, we do have to talk about the details—meals, clothes, chores—but we can't allow these things to keep us on the outside of a heart. When activities start eliminating sharing time, it's time to eliminate the activities.

Finally, we can miss the boat if we aren't prepared to take advantage of the opportunities that God provides. God is interested in deep relationships, but we have to pay attention. We want to get close to our children's hearts before they know there's an option.

___ Communicate the Vision ___

If you want a child who is healthy in heart (Proverbs 12:18), the words you use must constantly elevate your child's mind and heart. Your child needs to be on the high ground, and you can either help him get there or keep him away. Your words can be an encouragement to be victorious or reckless weapons that "pierce like a sword."

Where are your words taking your children?

Most of us can remember a special comment that someone made, an insight or encouragement that is as crystal clear now as when we first heard it. I remember a stranger in a restaurant who once told me I had a gift for speaking; whether true or not, it encouraged me to believe I could actually do something worthwhile from a pulpit or platform. Comments *can* plant or nurture a vision. Wouldn't it be something if your children had a long list of special things you said to think back on, even after you've gone?

But how many of us carry around a *crusher* instead—a brutal, devastating comment that made us rethink our whole value as a person? I have some of those; my guess is that you do, too. A single word can have such power!

Whether the memorable comment was positive or negative, the person giving it may not have even known the effect their statement had. This tells us two things: First, how closely we must guard every word; and second, how much better we could do if we actually *plan* to make memorable comments of the positive variety.

___ *Guard and Plan Your Words* ___

It's a very good thing for parents to involve their children in discussions about family finances. It helps to teach them that money doesn't grow on trees and can give them a way to be responsible in helping to trim one budget area (e.g., the light bill) so more can be spent elsewhere (e.g., the poor).

But there are so many ways for you to say things that will make your children feel they're a burden: "I can't believe these doctor bills!" "The school is raising tuition *again*." "I think I'm going to have to get a second job to support this bunch."

Picture yourself at age 80. And picture this comment: "I don't know how we'll ever get ahead with having to take care of Dad."

Doesn't sound so hot, does it? Guard your words.

And what about the planning of memorable words? Start by communicating your vision of parenting to your child. Let him know where you want him to be, *who* you want him to be. This *doesn't* mean you put a lot of pressure on your child to be something that he isn't able to be. That can and will discourage him. If math and science don't register, don't push him to be a nuclear physicist.

But all children can and should be pushed to be godly. Nobody who has the Holy Spirit is unqualified here. Let your children know that God and you are negotiable on the details of life, but not on the vision "that you may be filled to the measure of all the fullness of God" (Ephesians 3:19).

This may seem beyond your ability. It is. Certainly, the realm of parenting the next generation of God's own is no place for the faint of heart. But remember, you're not going to do this in your own strength. With God's wisdom and power, which He has promised over and over to give us in abundance, you can accomplish this.

God *wants* you to succeed in this endeavor. He'll help you.

__ Use Your Own Life __

Anyone who speaks, teaches, or preaches knows the value of illustrations and examples to highlight the point he's trying to make. This is true with your children as well. They need to know the rock-solid reality of the Word of God and how it always proves itself out in practice. Biographies, news items, and articles can all be used in your effort to communicate truth to your children.

But you want to do more than communicate truth. You want to crawl inside a heart.

It may sound easier than it really is. Most of us are afraid that being vulnerable will somehow allow our children to see that we are not a bastion of perfection. Well, we usually *haven't* been a bastion of perfection, so we might as well give up the charade. Incredibly, they'll respect us *more*, not less.

Nothing will be more powerful in reaching inside the citadel of another heart than using your own experiences, feelings, and memories to reach inside and touch those same things inside your child's heart. It's so personal and rich and deep—it's almost guaranteed to be effective.

The Good and the Bad

Tell them about mistakes you've made, what you've learned, and how God brought you through to higher ground. Tell them what things made you laugh or cry, and why you think it's so. Share the good memories of days gone by, the distinct recollections of when God unmistakably laid His hand on your life. Let them see that you have a heart of flesh and not a heart of stone (see Ezekiel 11:19).

On one of our recent vacations, my then 17-year-old-daughter Laura and I went out on an errand about 9 P.M. We started talking about life and more specifically about how my life could contain learning experiences for her. What an unexpected time for a deep-heart conversation! I sketched out for her the decisions I had made and the paths I had taken over the past 20 years. I told her softly and candidly about times when I either was not listening to God very well, or I had not taken the time to make sure I was hearing His whole heart on a matter. We talked about the tough lessons I had learned, as well as seeing how God used those incidents in my training in spite of myself.

Many fathers are afraid of doing this with their children. They're afraid of being known, afraid of vulnerability, afraid that this will somehow reduce their "authority" or "respect" within the family. How unsure of ourselves and our positions we can be! If we only knew how doing this can cement relationships and increase our children's respect for us and our authority!

Laura and I also talked about some of those awesome, crystal-clear moments when God had moved in my life in a powerful way—my visions, my dreams, who I *really* am on the inside. Finally, I shared with her about a number of important relationships in my life (discerning children can see how these are going, so you might as well be open with them). I wanted her to know how some had gone sour, why they had gone that way, and what I could have done to change that. I wanted her to see the few special ones up close so she could see their value, learn how to solidify and treasure one, and learn how problems in a good relationship can be used to help *build* rather than tear down the love.

We talked until 2 A.M. They were five of the best hours I've ever spent "parenting." But without a willingness to share openly and simply, the whole conversation could have lasted 15 minutes and been worth very little on an eternal measuring scale. If I can do it long and deep, my friend, so can you.

Why is this so effective? For one thing, "parents are the pride of their children" (Proverbs 17:6), so what you were and are is important to them. And you have to understand that your children are yours by *design* (see Acts 17:26). Your life and experiences and feelings and memories are going to impact your children in ways that will reach very few others.

Many of us are afraid that being vulnerable will somehow allow our children to see that we are not a bastion of perfection. Well, we usually haven't been a bastion of perfection, so we might as well give up the charade.

Some cautions are in order. First, don't wallow around in the past (see Ecclesiastes 5:20). That won't do you or your children any good. Second, don't share certain things at all (see 1 Corinthians 14:20). You know in your own heart what I mean; some things just need to be forgotten, washed away forever by the blood of the Lamb. Third, present carefully the details you do bring into the open, and don't share some details at all (see Ecclesiastes 8:5). Finally, don't glorify your past: "Do not say, 'Why were the old days better than these?' For it is not wise to ask such questions" (Ecclesiastes 7:10).

Three-Minute Truths

Perhaps you're thinking you've got to have long conversations in order to get your hearts to touch. Don't let Satan lay that one on you. This feeling of "lots or nothing at all" can devastate your life in many ways, and parent-child communication is no exception. It doesn't have to be a big deal in order to be effective. Just three minutes can be plenty, if it's the right three minutes. Let me illustrate.

One of the worst things we can give our children is a sense that their early lives are disposable, that those years are to just be enjoyed and spent on themselves. Nothing can seem further away to our children than old age and death, and our culture does everything it can to deny those twin realities.

I want my children to understand the brevity of life, the urgency of running a good race all the way through, and how things come full circle, with the weak becoming strong and then becoming weak again. I want them to have a sense of passing time, of generations coming and then fading away, of the intimate connection they have with their own older years.

I could say all of those things to my children in any number of long, in-depth discussions on life. But there's no better way than to look down the road with them with just a simple comment. For example:

- "You know, honey, I got to carry you in from the car last night and tuck you into bed. When I'm older and fall asleep in the car, will you carry me in and tuck me into bed?"

- "Do you enjoy it when I read you a bedtime story? You know, some day many years from now we may trade places, and I might be looking forward to your reading me a story at bedtime."

Believe me, your children won't laugh at you when you share thoughts like these—they'll esteem you all the more. And you've passed along important truths in under three minutes.

Avoid Leading Questions

As parents, some of us would qualify as frustrated

Perry Masons. We envision ourselves imparting knowledge and wisdom to our children by leading them through
a complex maze of questions that have only one correct
answer. After our brilliant cross-examination our sons
and daughters gasp, "I see, I see," and collapse in an
exhausted, but enlightened, heap. You feel very good,
have a nice victory under your belt, and plan on being
back at the same time next week.

But your children might not tune in.

A leading question is a question that leads to a single,
expected answer. It's almost a rhetorical question, except that it calls for a canned answer drawn from a well-
trained memory bank. It's the right approach if you're
trying to produce a "quiz kid" who knows the answers,
but it can be a disaster if you care about *why* he knows
them. Children are smarter than you might think.
They'll know if you're asking leading questions, and
they'll learn how to answer them to satisfy you.

Instead of asking, "Did Christ die for your sins?"
how about, "Why do you think some believe that Christ
died for their sins and others don't?" In place of the
predictable answer to the question "Is evolution true?"
imagine the possible dialogue created by "Will you
explain why *you* believe either creation or evolution is
true?"

Wording is *critical*. Never, ever, build the answer into
your questions. The best answers will come when your
children aren't completely sure which answer will please
you. Even wrong answers can be an excellent base for
future learning. If you never get a wrong answer or one
that shows some uncertainty on the part of your children, you're probably not asking very good questions.

Watch the tone of your questions as well. Children
very often get more from the tone of questions than the
questions themselves. If you ask even a very good question with different intonations and emphases, you can
cue your children on the "right" answer. Also, try

to avoid leading the answer with nods, interruptions, groans, and grimaces. This stuff can kill a good answer to a good question nine times out of ten. Just ask the question as best you can, and then try not to run over the answer.

Goethe's advice is appropriate: "What you have inherited from your fathers, earn over again for yourselves, or it will not be yours." This is serious business if you want to have children who are truly grounded in the Word of God and don't simply have the "right" answers. Your children need to own truth for themselves. You can be indispensable in their development of godliness, or you can steamroll them with the weight of your relentless, surefire questions.

___ *"Talk About Them"* ___

"Impress them on your children. Talk about them when you sit at home and when you walk along the road, when you lie down and when you get up" (Deuteronomy 6:7). This suggestion is pretty radical, but if used wisely it will boost your child's spiritual wisdom and strength dramatically.

Do you remember the story about the children trying to hang around Jesus? The apostles, operating under the "children shouldn't be seen *or* heard" school of child management, tried their best to get the little pests out of the conversation. After all, children wouldn't get much out of the important teachings of Jesus, would they?

How often do we react to children in the same way? Much too much, I'm afraid. We sit them at separate tables when families get together and hurry them out of the room so that we can have some undoubtedly weighty and crucial adult conversations. In effect, we deny them access to truly meaningful dialogue.

Children, among themselves, rarely have discussions of eternal value. Even if they wanted to, most of them aren't experienced enough or wise enough to make such conversation possible. So instead of sending them along on their merry little ways to play in the sand and stick gum in each other's hair and talk about Joey's big ears, we should let them grow—*insist* that they grow— by listening to the conversations of Christian adults.

We talk about some fairly unimportant things endlessly, not having the good sense to know when we have said enough. And we don't talk about some fairly important things at all.

Some of the best of these conversations can occur after a meeting at your church. You've just been stimulated spiritually, and you might be able to ask a good question or make an incisive comment to get a valuable conversation going. When this happens, you've created the perfect environment in which your children can grow.

You may have noticed that children often are interested in joining adult conversations. When something is important enough to command the attention, even excitement, of people they know and love and respect, the subject will generally grab their attention. It can even be irresistible. Children shouldn't be involved in all conversations, of course, but I do think our orientation ought to change from "What are these kids doing here?" to "Is there any legitimate reason why the kids shouldn't be listening to this?"

You'll find this to be an excellent vehicle for teaching children about important things in an indirect and non-challenging way. This isn't a minor exercise; *this is very important for their development.*

Suppose your child likes to wander off from where you told him to be. Disciplining the child is vital and must be done. But look at the possible effectiveness in bringing up, with some Christian friends, the dangers of being in the wrong place. Have your friends share some of their bad experiences from childhood or adulthood, and you share yours. Share with each other what you learned from God about these things.

My experience says that real people talking about real learning experiences will outweigh a good lecture or spanking by five to one. It's powerful teaching because it's *real* to the children.

So go out tonight and talk a little with your family and friends. *And take the kids.*

__ Spend Time Together __

Part of excellent communication is being there for the little times, the everyday happenings and comments. The most important thing is not that you fill up your time together with conversation, but that you're there to listen and observe and share life together. Then, as God and circumstances lead, spend a few minutes crawling into a heart. You may need four hours of quantity time to get three minutes of quality. If you're only there for an hour of quantity time, you may not get any quality time at all.

Have some things to say and ask when these quality times occur. From your own observations: "We only see one side of that pretty moon. I wonder why God designed it that way?" Or regarding his or her interests: "I think it's neat how you like to work with wood. I wonder why Jesus was a carpenter instead of something else?" Simple thoughts and simple questions.

Be there to ask them.

Outings

No matter how much other quantity and quality time you try to have with your children at home, you need to consider establishing a practice with each of your children that will allow your relationship to grow deeper. Having a regular outing with each of your children individually is one of the most effective methods of discipling available to parents, yet I personally know of few parents who are doing it. Honestly, this is the easiest thing that you will ever do. It's even *fun*, as long as you don't trip over your own seriousness.

People have asked me at what age this activity should be started. I was 27, so that certainly isn't too young. (Oh, and my older daughter was two-and-a-half.) We talked about it for several days ahead of time, but I wasn't sure if she knew what we were going to do (in fact, *I* wasn't really sure). I came home to find that she'd insisted on dressing up in her Sunday finest for Daddy, and we went out and had the time of our lives.

We have continued to try to do so on a monthly basis ever since. We have missed some, but we always try to make it a priority. After all these years, this daughter has developed an interesting philosophy: Since it's natural to talk about problems and challenges with me, she can't understand why anyone wouldn't ask her own dad for advice or help. Indeed.

What you do isn't as important as the fact that you're doing it together, but here are some ideas:

- Go for a walk (preferably a long one).
- Go to dinner (hot dogs are fine—it doesn't have to be expensive).
- Go to the movies, the theater, a ballet, a concert, a ball game, the museum (and make sure you allow time over dessert afterward to have a discussion).
- Go window-shopping.
- Go shopping for something for someone whom you both love.
- Do a project together.

Don't just think about or talk about this outing idea. Do it. Tonight wouldn't be too soon to start.

Send Notes

This thought allows you to spend time with your children when you're apart. Send your own children notes in the mail—not only when you're on trips, but when you're at work, too. Write these notes when things are quiet and you can say something tender and vulnerable and memorable. Everybody likes to get personal notes. They can be read over and over and saved and treasured.

And don't just put these notes on your child's dresser. Be a big spender and put stamps on them and really mail them.

It could be the best work the post office has done for you in years.

___ *Enough's Enough* ___

"Having a good conversation is like taking a good vacation; it helps to know where to stop."

I don't remember who said it; it's certainly true. But I think the more serious problem is not in saying too much, but rather in saying too little. More to the point, we talk about some fairly unimportant things endlessly, not having the good sense to know when we have said enough. And we don't talk about some fairly important things at all.

"These commandments that I give you today are to be upon your hearts. Impress them on your children. Talk about them when you sit at home and when you walk along the road, when you lie down and when you get up" (Deuteronomy 6:6-7). We are supposed to be talking about life and faith all the time. You get the picture that God wants this particular family activity pretty high on your priority list as parents.

But just talking about the Word of God won't cut the mustard. You're supposed to *impress* these things on your children. You are to teach your children to love the Lord their God with all their hearts and all their souls and all their strength. God is quite clear that this is made easier if *you* love the Lord your God with all your heart and soul and strength. And act like you do.

Not talking enough includes areas other than Scripture. We don't talk enough about our:

- *Experiences.* Your kids really take pride in you. They'll delight in hearing about the many ways that God has worked in your life.

- *Mistakes.* Your children don't have enough time to make all of the mistakes of which they are capable. Hearing about yours can save them a lot of grief, in addition to giving you both (if you're big enough) a good laugh.

- *Values.* We usually have some, but we don't describe them very well, nor do we take the time to give our kids some practical applications of these values. Tell them *why* you think something is important, some ways you practice this, and give them some ways they can try it out. Then let them see the results.

- *Friends.* Your kids can already tell much about you by the company you keep. Tell them why you spend time with each of your friends. If you're helping someone who has a lot of problems and is not a close friend, tell your children about that, too.

- *Work, school, and other activities.* Many of us are silent about how we spend the better, or at least longer, part of our time. Not bringing work home is a good practice, but this should not mean that you don't even talk about it.

Of course, there is such a thing as talking too much. Most of us like to babble, and we are much too prone to nag our children long after we have made our point and good sense has disappeared from the conversation.

Scripture has a memorable verse that isn't addressed specifically to parents, but it seems to have some of them in mind: "Even a fool is thought wise if he keeps silent, and discerning if he holds his tongue" (Proverbs 17:28).

Talk enough about the things of God and you'll become more than parent and child. You'll become rich, deep, exquisite, and delightful friends, and this friendship will be passed by your young friend to his young friends—to the third and fourth generations.

We Interrupt — This Broadcast . . . —

"He who answers before listening—that is his folly and his shame" (Proverbs 18:13).

If someone wants to drive us up the wall, one of the surest ways to do it is to interrupt us when we are talking. It says to us that what we're saying isn't very important. If it's done to us often enough, we can start questioning the worth of what we are saying and resent the one who obviously thinks so little of us.

I'm amazed at how many parents allow their children to interrupt them while the parents are talking directly to them. Worse still is the constant interruption of adult conversations by these small human beings, who may be operating under the delusion that they are the center of the universe. Parents can fall for this, and children can play them for all they're worth.

From lengthy studies done by this writer while driving on interstate highways, it is a fact that the world is full of rude people. Don't let your child add to that statistic. *Never* let him interrupt you or anyone else, unless it's an absolute emergency. When he tries, hold up your finger in front of his face, and make eye contact and shake your head if necessary. (If he's having trouble letting you know he's there—usually unlikely—you can allow him to tap you on the arm, *once*.) Always make him wait until the conversation is at a stopping point or finished, and then allow him to make his announcement.

Consistency in this matter is absolutely crucial for success. You might be tempted to restrain him if the conversation is important, but let him interrupt if it's trivial. But you'll only confuse him, since he might not know whether your conversation is important or not. It's *always* important, though, that he knows that interruptions are *never* trivial.

As with other things, you'll have to set the pace in this area by not interrupting others. This includes other adults in conversations, and even harder, it includes not interrupting children in their *own* conversations. It's all too easy for us to assume that their dialogue isn't very important. Shame on us.

Take Time to Listen

There's another side to this idea of interruptions. It's when we are so uninterested in a conversation that we are distracted by anything and everything around us. It can get to the point where we *want* someone or something to interrupt our conversation. But is there anything more maddening than talking to someone who listens with only token interest?

And then there's our children.

We can be so tired or so busy or so not wanting to be bothered that we can turn almost our entire relationship with our kids into one big "token." It's particularly easy when they're little, and the things that are so important to them are so truly trivial to us—"Mommy, look at the wonderful doll I made out of this disposable diaper"; "Daddy, look at this leaf I found squashed under your snow tires." To be honest, these things really *aren't* important—not to us, not to others, not at all. They're only important to our children.

But that's enough. These things are important because your *child* is important. They're part of his life and growth, and he has a God-given desire to share these discoveries with you. If you listen when they're little, they'll still be talking to you when the subjects *are* important.

Get rid of all this half-listening, half-paying attention while your child is sharing with you. Eliminate the "uh huh" while you continue washing dishes or reading the newspaper. You might not think that these things are discourteous, but they are. When you listen with token interest, you've given your child part of your ear and none of your heart.

When your child approaches you, say either, "Okay, let's talk about it," or "I can't give you my full attention right now, but you deserve it, so let's talk in an hour." Adjust the time delay appropriately; for younger ones, an hour might seem like a month.

One important caution. When you actually start listening, you're going to hear some things you disagree with. But don't sail into their words. Don't respond harshly or without thinking. And don't interrupt to make your own points. Scripture says, "He who answers before listening—that is his folly and his shame" (Proverbs 18:13). Too many of us can produce about 200 cases of folly and shame in a 20-minute conversation.

We should at least listen to our own flesh and blood as we would listen to an interesting dinner guest. If you do this, when your child is an adult, he may still *be* one of your interesting dinner guests.

Make Yourself Available

All of the tips in the world won't make you a better parent or your child a better person if you don't spend a lot of raw time on the effort. One of the popular ideas in our society is that it's the quality of time, not the quantity of time, that matters.

Sounds good, doesn't it?

Now, I have no argument with the fact that time spent with children should be of very high quality. Nothing is of higher quality than teaching your child about God and His Word, and Scripture tells us we should be doing this all day long (see Deuteronomy 6:7-9).

But if you're trying to be a parent who works his craft with any kind of skill at all, you must spend a *lot* of quality time with your children. Just as a person can leave a more lasting mark on a profession by his intensity and length of service, so a parent can leave a more lasting mark on his child. There is no substitute for just being available.

How many children—how many of *us*—have been stifled in a potentially exquisite relationship with parents who ended too many conversations with a hard, cold "Not now"? Or "Can't you see I'm busy?" Or "Don't you have anything else to do?" Too many of us. And when we and they are older, how many of us will hear, from those we rebuffed so many years before, another hard, cold "Not now"?

Everyone is born with "holes" in their hearts. The big hole in the center can only be filled by God. But there are other holes: a "man-sized" hole that can be filled by a daddy, and a "woman-sized" hole that can be filled by a mommy. If a daddy or mommy won't make themselves available, the hole just aches, and all too often gets "filled" by the wrong kind of person. The hole can widen until it seems unfillable.

Some parents' lack of availability has allowed great harm to come upon their children. If there is sexual abuse involved, your "not now" could push your child away at the very time he or she needs you most. You'll have to go well beyond just saying, "Not now." You'll have to peer into his countenance, seize the moment, and probe his heart to discover the abuse. It won't be easy for him to talk about it. You'll have to help. And you will already have had to create the trust that will allow him to share.

Next time your child asks you to do something with him, do one thing before you tell him "Not now." Just look into his eyes for 15 seconds. Look deep and look hard. Force yourself to realize that this time, this request, this need will never come again.

___ *Don't Lecture; Listen* ___

Not too long ago, I saw a great line in a Father's Day card: "If I didn't have you, Dad . . . I'd have to lecture myself."

Why do most of us lecture when instead we could help our children to teach themselves? When a child brings you an idea or request that you think he hasn't thought through, or that you simply disagree with, or that really is the dumbest thing you ever heard, don't jump into a lecture. This knee-jerk response will teach him not to ask you any questions at all, even when you really want him to. Besides that, he'll understand more certainly if he lets God's Spirit tell his spirit, rather than if you just impose an answer on him.

For example, your 16-year-old son has asked if he can hitchhike to New Orleans and catch a tramp steamer to the Bahamas, where he intends to spend a year working odd jobs on the beach. If you say, "That's the dumbest idea I've ever heard," you've blown it. Even if you win and he doesn't actually go, you've blown it.

Your boy has given you a marvelous opportunity to help him learn how to *think*, and you've used it as an opportunity to exhibit your power. What happens in eight years when he has another fabulously ridiculous idea, but isn't taking your orders anymore?

Be different. Take some time and really listen to your son.

Listen to the Strong Points

Start by asking your son to explain the strong points of his idea or position. Probe with questions that honestly seek to know. He'll have to do some more thinking, and it might even be that *you'll* learn something. In fact, if you give yourself and him a chance, you might even change your *own* opinion on the subject.

Junior might tell you that he could learn how to take care of himself if he were to leave home and go to the Bahamas. The beaches and surf will be like heaven on earth to him, and he'll be able to learn a lot about sand. He might even shuffle his feet and suggest that he could do some real missionary work while he's surfing.

Quietly listening at this point could land you in the Parental Hall of Fame, alongside the other five parents in history who actually had the humility to believe they could learn something from their own kids. And you could stop the conversation here, but don't do it. Keep going.

Listen to the Weak Points

Move on to the weak points of his argument. Now it'll be hard to get yourself out of the way and stay there when he starts talking. After all, you might think, *I'm so smart and he's so dumb . . . er, young. Wouldn't it be better just to point out the weak points myself, and nail him . . . er, it to the wall?*

No.

Ask *him* to point out the weak points himself. He might tell you that he could be placing himself in danger by hitchhiking or catching the tramp steamer, or that he'll miss the family and church and friends he has at home. He might suggest that taking a break in his education could ruin his college or career plans. With a little gentle prodding, he might even confess that his real intention was to do more surfing than sharing.

Help him do this, but don't do it for him. As he works his way through it, you might be absolutely *amazed* at how smart he is, how thorough, how delightfully excited to be allowed the courtesy of thinking. You might even start a whole habit of thoughtfulness in your child. Radical!

Cautions

Two cautions are in order. First, don't pounce on your child's weak points with heartless gusto. If you do, you'll eliminate this wonderful tool from your workbench. Honest discussion, seasoned with a generous amount of humility, can be one of his and your most rewarding disciplines. If you need help on your humility, just remember some of the strange things you thought about when *you* were younger.

Second, always make sure that you let this young soul save face. Don't play sportscaster and insist on being concerned with who wins. Jesus wasn't concerned about winning *arguments*; He was concerned about winning *hearts*. Allow your child the opportunity to withdraw his request or idea and to believe that he learned to withdraw it on his own.

By doing this, you won't have to defend your own position. This "defending" can be very hard to do well, especially if your child isn't listening or if you haven't thought through all the fine points. But if you're like many parents, not having to continually defend your position is a definite plus.

Your kids will think so, too.

___ *Don't Ignore Evil* ___

Many adults talk to their children as though life is a coin with the same image on both sides. No matter which way things are flipped, "heads" always comes up. Perhaps if we are honest, we'd admit that we would prefer not to have to distinguish between heads and tails ourselves. Or sometimes we feel our faith isn't strong enough to deal with challenges to it.

Whatever the reason, we often simply teach that heads is not only right, but that it's the only choice. But if heads is so obviously right, why are we so afraid to show our children the other side of the coin? It has one, you know, and someone will be glad to show it to them. Why not you?

The odds of true gray areas appearing are about the same as the odds of a coin landing on its side. The Bible talks about "One Lord . . . ; one God and Father of all, who is over all and through all and in all" (Ephesians 4:5-6). There's only one truth, and everything not true is a lie. There's no middle ground, at least not if we believe what the Bible says about lukewarm things (Revelation 3:15-16).

Caution, of course, must be exercised when you begin to show your children the other side of the coin. One way to arouse the wrong kind of curiosity is to shower children with too much detail about the other side of the coin. We don't need to have our heads in the sewer to know that sewage stinks.

Another way is to tell your children too much too soon. We need to be especially careful not to lay things that have been problems for us on our children before they're ready to use the information properly. Protect their spirits. Too much information given too soon is too much visibility for the other side of the coin.

There's a third and final way that's fairly certain to arouse this curiosity in your children. Try to convince them that the other side of the coin doesn't exist at all.

Be Prepared

I've been told that some U.S. agents become experts at picking out counterfeit bills by studying only the real thing. That's an admirable method. But you better believe that these same agents also know that there *are* counterfeit bills, why people make them, and what they're used for. They know about real money *and* about the dangers of counterfeiting.

Your children must learn from you about the truth *and* about the counterfeits and their dangers—who believes the lie, why they believe it, and the results of such misplaced belief.

Jesus warned His people to be ready, to be prepared to deal with the great lies that are inevitable in an evil world. He said:

> Watch out that no one deceives you. For many will come in my name, claiming, "I am the Christ," and will deceive many. . . . If anyone says to you, "Look, here is the Christ!" or, "There he is!" do not believe it. For false Christs and false prophets will appear and perform great signs and miracles to deceive even the elect—if that were possible (Matthew 24:4-5,23-24).

Jesus was obviously concerned about His people being unprepared and gullible, having no understanding of who and what evil is or how to deal with it. He taught us about the other side of the coin, not as an exercise or just to show He was wise, but *because He loved us and wanted us to be ready*. We should do no less for our children.

Teach the Truth

You must teach what the Bible and history teach about life, and also what they teach about death. Without both sides of the coin, your children will be ignorant, unprepared, gullible, and caught off guard by something that has no power except its power to deceive.

Teaching your children the truth includes teaching them that certain things are lies, because *it's true that these things are lies.* Don't be afraid to grab hold of the lies by the neck, to expose them by the light of God and His Word.

The church in the nineteenth century tried to ridicule the new "science" of Darwin and others without trying to understand it or develop scientific arguments against it. The church was steamrolled. You will be too, if you can't make an intelligent defense of your faith after you've done an intelligent job of analyzing and explaining the other side.

If there are questions raised about your beliefs, let your children see them and work with you to resolve them. Let them see that you're open to truth no matter what the source or where you find it. Look together at the strong points and weak points of both sides of the coin. And never stop before you both commit your hearts to the side of truth, even if all the details aren't clear or can't yet be fully explained.

This is the approach, for example, that many Christians are using today to explain the origins of man. Looking at the evolution side as well as the creation side strengthens the power of the creation viewpoint, even as it shows evolution to be one of the great lies of modern times.

And guess who's been caught this time, stuttering and stammering, teaching that, in this case, the coin has only one side? You guessed it.

It's not us.

___ *The Art of Rebuking* ___

"Better is open rebuke than hidden love" (Proverbs 27:5).

Are You serious, Lord? I'm sure You realize that this rebuke business can hurt the old ego, don't You, Lord? Do You really mean it?

You bet He does.

God wants us to be transparent in our relationships with all people: men, women, children, believers, unbelievers. He wants us to love openly and, hard as it may be, to rebuke those who need it for *their* benefit, *because we love them.*

Rebuke Versus Criticism

Bernard Baruch said that we should never answer a critic, unless he's right. The first thing to teach your children is the difference between *rebuke* and *criticism*. *Criticism* is the highlighting of either good or bad points about a person or thing. Theoretically, it can be used to make someone or something better; in practice, however, it's most often used to tear someone or something down. Your children need to learn to reject criticism— unless, of course, it's true.

What is *rebuke*? According to Webster's, to *rebuke* is "to reprehend sharply." But in God's scheme of things, rebuke of another human being is the loving, caring attempt to restore him to solid footing on God's path. Your children must learn to accept your rebuke. Nothing less will move them toward their potential, nothing less will teach them how to accept rebuke, and nothing less will teach them how to properly rebuke others.

First, your rebuke of your children must be wise to be effective. Scripture says, "Like an earring of gold or an ornament of fine gold is a *wise* man's rebuke to a listening ear" (Proverbs 25:12). You must ask yourself: *Is this rebuke? Or is this just nagging?*

Second, your rebuke must be faithful. Scripture says, "Faithful are the wounds of a friend" (Proverbs 27:6, NASB). This certainly implies that your wounds, your rebuke, must be consistent; but there's more to it. It's also telling us that the rebuke must be full of faith, prompted by your faith, and centered around the idea of encouraging faithfulness in your child.

Third, your rebuke must be given in love, following Jesus' example: "Those whom I love I rebuke" (Revelation 3:19). Remember that only a friend's wounds are faithful—the rest just hurt. Jesus rebuked His apostles and followers *because* He loved them.

Fourth, your rebuke should only relate to sin on the part of your child. Jesus said, "If your brother sins, rebuke him" (Luke 17:3). Don't take on such an awesome duty for trivial things. Make it appropriate. Learn the difference between rebuking and nitpicking.

Fifth, your rebuke of your child should go right along with correction and encouragement, "with great patience and careful instruction" (2 Timothy 4:2). You want to let the child know that he's out of line, but you also want to show him the correct way and encourage him to run on that path. The call for great patience eliminates the idea of rebuking in a rage, and the call for careful instruction means you should actually *plan* the rebuke.

Paul reminds us,

> The Lord's servant must not quarrel; instead, he must be kind to everyone [even children!], able to teach, not resentful. Those who oppose him [even children!] he must gently instruct, in the hope that God will grant them repentance leading them to a knowledge of the truth, and that they will come to their senses and escape from the trap of the devil (2 Timothy 2:24-26).

If your rebuke follows this pattern, you can test your child's level of wisdom by his reaction to your rebuke. If your rebuke gets you hate, he's a mocker; if it gets you love, he's wise (see Proverbs 9:8). In fact, this is really all the test that you need, since "a mocker does not listen to rebuke" (Proverbs 13:1), but "a rebuke impresses a man of discernment" (Proverbs 17:10).

Rebuke and Church Authority

> If your brother sins against you, go and show him his fault, just between the two of you. If he listens to you, you have won your brother over. But if he will not listen, take one or two others along, so that "every matter may be established by the testimony of two or three witnesses." If he refuses to listen to them, tell it to the church (Matthew 18:15-17).

Your children deserve to be beneficiaries of this Scripture.

Mom, if you have a problem with your children, try to work it out with them and leave Dad out of it. If you get results, stop there. If you don't, then bring Dad in.

And what if you both fail to get a response from your child? What if your child hardens his heart against your authority? Then "tell it to the church." What? *The church?* Yes. Your pastors and elders are there—or should be there—to help you with the nuts and bolts of your family life.

What's the basis for this?

> If a man has a stubborn and rebellious son who does not obey his father and mother and will not listen to them when they discipline him, his father and mother shall take hold of him and bring him to the elders at the gate. . . . Then all the men of his town shall stone him to death. You must purge the evil from among you (Deuteronomy 21:18-21).

"Stoning" can involve rebuke by the elders, assistance to the family in the area of rules and discipline, and in extreme cases, discipline by the elders and even excommunication from the church. The family is to accept this and choose to honor God and His Word. If you have a problem with this because it's an Old Testament passage, please note that Jesus, in Matthew 18, also uses an Old Testament passage. Do you think that God no longer considers rebellion against parents an evil to be purged?

This is pretty tough. But holiness is tough. Parenting is tough. Parenting without the help of your church's shepherds is very tough. Involve your leaders when you need them, even if you have to drag them in, kicking and screaming.

Excellent Communication ___ *Starts Now* ___

We've covered a lot in this chapter. Excellent communication with your children is not easy. It's complicated. It takes time. And it's a lot of work. It certainly won't happen overnight, but it won't happen at all if you don't make a commitment now to get started.

You can do it. Talk to your kids. Crawl inside their hearts.

4

The Power of an Excellent Example

Fiction: You can't do anything to make your children adopt your values.

Fact: Everyone who is fully trained will be *like* his teacher (Luke 6:40).

This is where the rubber meets the road.

My dad used to tell me, "Don't do as I do, do as I say." Maybe some of you heard this from your parents as well. Even when parents don't say this, it is often the way they live out their lives.

You might just as well try to convince your children that they hate getting presents or going on vacation. The Scripture says that "parents are the pride of their children" (Proverbs 17:6); for better or worse, this means that your children are going to be like you *are*, not like you *say*. The ideal, of course, is that what you are and what you say are the same thing—godly.

But beyond the simple fact that your children are going to imitate you—good and bad, decent and indecent, worthwhile and trivial—is another simple fact: Jesus says that a fully trained disciple is one who is just like his teacher.

This "being just like" can work against you. You're deluding yourself if you think that your life isn't an open book before your children. While you can hide some of your bad actions, they'll pick up your responses, your looks, the way you spend and prioritize your time, the edges of your sloppy ways. According to Scripture, what's really in there will come out (see Luke 6:45). If the junk is there, sooner or later your kids will see it.

You have to make the decision to be godly yourself. That way, when you're all through training your children to be like you, it'll be worth writing home about.

The alternative to this destructive parenting is for you to actually *plan* to train your children to be just like you.

Kind of a scary thought, isn't it?

But that's the way you're going to get the result that you're looking for. That's the way Jesus trained His disciples—by showing them every day how to walk as He did. If you don't plan to have your child be just like you in spiritual values and understanding, you won't get it. It's just as simple as that.

Now it really gets scary.

You have to make the decision to *be* godly yourself. That way, when you're all through training your children to be like you, it'll be worth writing home about.

It's absolutely futile to try to develop a spiritual champion if you aren't one yourself. Nobody has ever been able to make it work, and you won't be the first. Your child may still grow up to be a man or woman of God, but it won't be because of you—it'll be in spite of you. If your child still achieves great things in the kingdom of God, people will look at you and look at him and say, "Wow, I wonder how he overcame *his* upbringing?"

So you're just going to have to give up the idea that you can lecture your children to greatness, all the while floating through life and cruising toward the Rapture. We can fool some people for a while, but we won't fool our kids. They live too close.

Everyone learns by example. You did. Your children do and will. If you apply God's principles, and let your children see the godly life and then hear the words, your children "will be mighty in the land" (Psalm 112:2). God guarantees it.

___ *The Unspoken Law* ___

What's the first step in setting an example for your children to follow? You've got to choose to be spiritually inquisitive.

All champions for Christ have been spiritually inquisitive—wanting to know more about God, His Word, and the life and world He created. They're on fire to find God's best and incorporate it into their lives.

Now, you might be saying to yourself, *most of the time I just don't feel like being spiritually inquisitive*. Well, that's the thing about it—most people don't feel like it, most of the time. Our enemy is constantly working to make us not feel like it. But you know what? It just doesn't matter if you *feel* like it or not. You can *choose* to be spiritually inquisitive.

And how do you go about it?

Most of us grew up understanding the kinds of questions that should never be asked. Though we would be hard-pressed to trace the origins of this spirit-crippling disease, we most certainly have it, and just as certainly are passing it on to the next generation. The way this disease works is that our children can't ask the same questions that we couldn't ask, plus others we may have added to the list.

Most questions, though, deserve to be answered, *need* to be answered; and yet the very best and most important of them are often the ones that are left unspoken.

You need to overcome this handicap before you can help your children.

Take a Voyage of Discovery

Wake up! Montesquieu told us, "Slavery is ever preceded by sleep."

Begin to question, try to look at things—all things— from God's different and fresh perspectives. Your own example will be the best teaching you can provide to your children. Don't hide your children from a godly question that lurks in your heart, for the sake of maintaining the image of total knowledge and invincibility that you know (and that your children will someday surely find out) is a lie. Quit pretending you already have all the answers.

Let your children see the things you're searching through. They'll not only learn that it's all right to ask these questions, but they'll also learn how to find the answers as you pore over the Word of God—for only there are there any answers worth finding. God's operative principle is, "Ask and it will be given to you. . . . For everyone who asks receives" (Matthew 7:7-8). He elaborates on this when He tells us, "If any of you lacks wisdom, he should *ask God*, who gives generously to all without finding fault, and it will be given to him" (James 1:5).

And don't be afraid to ask your own spiritual leaders for help in answering your questions. Scripture says, "He who walks with the wise grows wise" (Proverbs 13:20). Your children don't know everything, and—this may come as a shock—neither do you. You want your children to ask *you* for help and to follow your example of inquisitiveness. What better way to do this than for *you* to ask for help in this area and to follow another's example of inquisitiveness?

Encourage Questions

Finally, encourage your children to question and look into things for themselves. Make no issue completely out of bounds: not sin or death or fear or anger or sex or why you live the way you do or the effectiveness of prayer, to name just a few. Let them know that you value the desire to learn and grow that prompted their question.

Children *will* get answers to these questions; they *have* to, just to function. The real question is whether you're going to have any input, and the answer is totally up to you. If they never ask the questions, they'll be spiritual dwarves; if they only ask others who have never been trained to ask or learn, they won't be spiritual anythings.

After some probing on my part, I found out that my eight-year-old son David wanted to know why certain boys thought and talked so much about sexual things, especially when it made him "feel bad" to hear them. He wanted to know what he should say and do when they brought these things up or tried to get him into acting something out.

By getting him to ask the questions, I had David's attention in a special and penetrating way. I was answering what was important to him. I was addressing the questions he actually had on his mind, and not ones that he wasn't yet ready to ask. Our discussion led to some simple, nondramatic conversation about the purpose of sex and where babies come from.

You're probably going to have to work a little to get your kids to ask their questions. When you know they're thinking about something, or *ought* to be thinking about something, *don't* let the opportunity pass and *don't* ask the question yourself. Instead, reread the passage or restate the issue, and then ask them this: "Does this make you want to ask a question?"

Then have the good sense and patience to wait until they do. Don't be bothered if they don't ask what you were thinking of. First learn from their questions, and then let them learn from yours.

In my experience with counseling other people's children, I don't know what's been more frightening: the kinds of questions left unasked by so many young people until a very late age—questions about the nuts and bolts of living for God—or the fact that they didn't, or couldn't, ask their own parents.

___ *A Dad Without Honor* ___

The power of an excellent example can encourage your children to honor you and other authorities in their lives. Scripture has a very interesting promise, contingent upon a command: "Honor your father and your mother, as the LORD your God has commanded you, so that you may live long and that it may go well with you" (Deuteronomy 5:16). Paul finds this so important that he quotes it in the book of Ephesians and adds that this "is the first commandment with a promise" (6:2). God obviously thinks that family authority is of great importance.

"Boy," you say, "I'm glad you're getting into this. I really need to get this idea pounded into my child." This would be all right, if we parents weren't so hypocritical about this command.

Look again at the verse above. Does it say that "honoring" ends when we get married or for some legitimate reason have to move out of our parents' house? Do you see an age limit? What happens to us as *adults* when we follow this command?

And perhaps more to the point, what happens to us as adults when we *don't* follow it?

In giving this command, God uses words that allow and require this to be used throughout our lifetime. He expects us to honor our parents, without qualification, without age limit, without reservation of any kind. Paul, in Ephesians, adds the additional command for children to obey their parents, before he quotes the command to honor them. Even when we as adults are no longer in a position to *obey* our parents, we are always in a position to *honor* them.

So here's the point: If you aren't honoring your parents, how on earth can you expect *your* children to honor *you*? No teaching on respect for parents will be as powerful to them as watching you relate to your own parents. If you honor them, you're a long way in teaching their grandchildren to honor you.

How do you as a married adult honor your parents?

There are many, many ways. You can praise them publicly for their efforts with you and your children. You can ask them for advice and help on important matters. You can express your appreciation for all the times they cared for you and provided for you. You can tell them thanks for all the times they could have justifiably thrashed you and didn't. And you can avoid putting them into an institution when they're still able to be out and in your care.

And if you don't honor your parents, you have no right to expect anything more from your own children.

"But," you might say, "you don't know my parents!"

Even if your parents are the most degenerate people who ever lived, *this command applies to you*. You must do it regardless of their personalities or any circumstances, because God says so. There's no way around it, no matter how old you are, how far from their home, or how horrible they were. Nowhere in Scripture can you find God authorizing anyone to stop honoring his parents.

Honor your parents, even when they're obtuse and seem unworthy of honor. It's possible that your children will learn more about this principle when you honor such parents than when your parents appear worthy of such honor. To not do as your sinful parents do, and at the same time to show them honor and respect because God says so—now *that's* a powerful example.

So, parents, don't let your dads and moms be without honor. Follow the command, and watch your children follow you.

Men and Women __ Under Authority __

This same crucial idea carries over into your relationships with other authorities in your life. The focus here is on your relationship with church authority, although the principle applies elsewhere (for example, the authority in your vocation). Hebrews 13:17 says it pretty clearly: "Obey your leaders and submit to their authority. They keep watch over you as men who must give an account. Obey them so that their work will be a joy, not a burden, for that would be of no advantage to you."

Pretty straightforward, isn't it?

And yet, too many Christians just won't obey their church leaders and submit to their authority. People who insist that their children obey them because God says so, won't obey their own authority in the family of God because God says so.

It's just amazing how people can wander from church to church, picking and choosing, disregarding what is difficult, never obeying or submitting to anyone, and then expect instant obedience from their own children. Some parents openly criticize and even tear down church leaders in front of their children. Some people have even quit being a part of any church family.

If this describes you, did you ever wonder why your children pick and choose which instruction to obey and which to disregard? Did you ever think about why they chafe under your authority at times? Can you understand how your own disobedience can lead to a disobedient spirit in your children?

If you aren't a man or woman under authority, you're the reason your children might have big problems with your authority. Children might obey for a time by force, but they'll only learn the spirit of obedience by *example*.

Let your children see you do something you really don't want to do because you've been told by your spiritual authority to do it, and you can save many lectures. Tell your children about it: "You know, I didn't want to help that person, but Bill told me I should, so I did." Let them know that obedience isn't always fun, but that it *is* always mandatory, as long as the command doesn't contradict God's Word.

Surely we shouldn't do anything immoral or against God's Word, and leaders, like parents, can go too far in dictating the details of life to those under their authority. But these aren't the big problems in most of what today parades as Christianity. The big problems are that too many people don't want to obey things that are in line with God's Word.

For our sake, as well as our children's, we had better start obeying.

Who Will Take — Out the Trash? —

If you want godly children, you must be very careful about what they see you watching and what they hear you listening to.

Most Christians, and even many non-Christians, are very concerned about the kinds of things that their children might see or hear in this filthy culture. This is a totally legitimate concern. We must guard our children's spirits carefully and control the world's input.

There's so much garbage out there that is ready to seep in any crack, any opening. A wise parent will keep his children's spirits tightly shut up against this slimy reality and keep his spiritual caulking—the wisdom and power of God—handy at all times.

To those who say that we shouldn't overprotect our children or leave them unprepared to face the world, we should say, "God *put* me here to protect my children! I want them to face the world prepared with the wisdom of God, not the knowledge of the details of evil." Seeing and hearing trash won't make your children one iota stronger, but it will probably stunt their spiritual growth— or kill it altogether.

But guarding what your children see and hear is the bare *minimum* required to have a child who's spiritually surviving. What we're interested in here is what's needed to develop a child who is "mighty in the land" (Psalm 112:2).

In this area, as in all others, your best and worst teaching is going to come to your children by your example. While they're young, you can control their intake of information pretty well. But if you teach them something different by your example, all of your control will have been for nothing when they're old enough to make their own choices.

Because they're going to choose to be like you.

We are fond of talking in this country about "adult" and "children's" varieties of books, movies, music, and so on. There isn't any such distinction in the Word of God. He calls all of us to be like little innocent children in our faith and in our lack of knowledge of the evil that surrounds us. Although there are certain things that your children won't be ready to see or hear or learn at certain stages of their childhood, the question should not be, What should be allowed? but, What are they prepared for?

Timing of things, yes; *types* of things, no. In other words, you shouldn't watch or listen to anything without your children that you would be embarrassed about if they were present.

If it isn't edifying, and causing you to think on

"whatever is true...noble...right...pure...lovely...
admirable...excellent...or praiseworthy" (Philippians 4:8), then don't watch it or listen to it. Don't exercise your right to watch this corruption because you're over 18. *Act* like a mature adult and shut it out.

David says, in Psalm 101:

> I will walk *in my house* with blameless heart. I will set before my eyes no vile thing. ... I will have nothing to do with evil. ... My eyes will be on the faithful in the land. ... Every morning I will put to silence all the wicked in the land (verses 2-8).

If your children see you pouring garbage into your spirit, the battle is over. Guard them all you want—they'll still look with anticipation to enjoying the forbidden fruits when they're older. Avoid these things like a new outbreak of the bubonic plague. And teach your children that they should be avoided by *all* Christians—not just the little ones—because these things are ungodly and degenerate and destructive of spiritual health and power.

The advantage of this to your children, and the side benefit of this course to you, is a delightful one. You'll actually be able to walk with a pure heart. If you do this, Jesus said in the Sermon on the Mount that you and your children will see God (see Matthew 5:8).

And He, my friend, *is* worth watching.

___ Seventy Times Seven ___

Forgiveness is one of the hallmarks of Christianity and the healing lotion that helps deep wounds to become even deeper love. How many children have you ever seen actually go up to an adult or child whom they have offended and *on their own* ask his or her forgiveness? My guess is that many of us would honestly have to answer none.

Think about it. The whole gospel is based on the principle of godly sorrow that brings repentance and a plea to God for forgiveness (see 2 Corinthians 7:10), and yet we just don't see children practicing this with God *or* their peers. Something is missing in spirits that have no deep appreciation for walking in a forgiven state.

Jesus taught: "If you are offering your gift at the altar and there remember that your brother has something *against you*, leave your gift there in front of the altar. First go and be reconciled to your brother; then come and offer your gift" (Matthew 5:23-24).

That's pretty clear, and yet we can allow our children to run amok, ripping through their peers and other adults with razor-sharp tongues and cruel, thoughtless actions. This forgiveness principle is too serious to overlook.

If we do, the passage above indicates that God will not even bother to hear our children until they've cleaned out their unforgiven offenses (see Psalm 66:18).

So the bottom line, the foundation of a powerful relationship to God and the beginning of a successful walk with one's brothers and sisters in Christ, is based on actively seeking forgiveness. In our own lives, we must learn the importance of this action and keep short accounts with God and His people. With regard to our children, we must teach them to repent and seek forgiveness when necessary, because "repentance . . . leads to salvation" (2 Corinthians 7:10).

There, however, comes the dilemma. Any parent who has ever tried to force his little charges to ask forgiveness knows that it's a lot easier to get them to scrub their own ears. Asking forgiveness just doesn't come naturally. To do it from the heart is the first step of a supernatural walk on God's higher ground. It requires a supernatural response from a supernaturally trained heart.

You can't force them to do it. So how do you teach them to do it? Where is this supernatural training going to come from?

Surprise! You must show them by your example.

Teach by Example

Seeking forgiveness is so sensitive that it must be demonstrated for children to have any true idea of its importance. Teach them the Word of God on the subject, of course; this will be their basis for belief and practice of this principle throughout their lives. But if you want them to really know how to do it, and to actively pursue it, you're just going to have to give them an example to follow.

Unfortunately, it's very rare for a parent to ask forgiveness of someone else in the presence of a child (we could start with our spouses). We don't *like* to be humiliated and embarrassed, and that's how we usually perceive this particular action. And so we set an example of pride, refusing to seek forgiveness at all, much less in front of our child.

Even worse, our bitterness and anger toward the other person can spill out of our spirits and mouths. Don't be naive! If this describes you, your child will learn how to hold grudges and be bitter and angry, even as you mouth the words that Jesus wants him to seek forgiveness.

We must lay aside our pride and seek forgiveness in the presence of all involved people, including our children. We must ask forgiveness in a genuine, gentle, humble, nonrecriminating manner. Then our children can see the beauty of restoration as the wounds are bound up by God and relationships are restored. A powerful image will be implanted into their spirits—that seeking forgiveness is an undeniable truth that can and must be done.

Seek Forgiveness from Your Children

And now we've come to something even more rare. There's no way that anyone can honestly say he's never done anything to offend his children, but have you sought their forgiveness? Have you been unable to rest until this blot on your relationship is erased? Have you treated your own flesh as well as you might treat some casual acquaintance?

If your answer is yes, praise God. If it's no, you're wrong before your children and God. You need to straighten this out for your own sake, as well as the sake of your children—immortal souls made in the image and likeness of God and of no less importance regarding forgiveness than your friends.

Don't go tell your kids that you're sorry. Go to them with a broken heart, genuinely sorrowful that you have hurt someone so intimately precious to you. Make no excuses under any circumstances. Let them know that you hate what you did, that you repent of it, and never by God's grace intend to do it again. And then ask them for forgiveness and wait for them to give it to you. If you do this in a godly way, you *will* be closer to your children.

And there's the beauty of it: You'll not only have cleared your account with your children, but you'll also have taught them, in the most powerful and commanding way open to a parent, how to ask forgiveness. They may still balk and need encouragement in particular cases, but they'll know that it can be done and that it can end in a beautiful way, because someone they love and respect has walked the path before them and shown them the way.

I remember a time, when Laura was a little girl, I had overreacted to something she had done. My words and tone had said something I really didn't want her to carry around in her heart. But then the "justifications" came: She really *was* a little out of control; she hadn't asked *my* forgiveness; I was tired and stressed and needed a little more understanding from my family; asking her forgiveness might somehow lower her opinion of me.

But God cut through all of that, pierced my heart, and told me to go do it. And so I did. It was a little awkward. I think I even had to help her remember and sort out the details (and fight the temptation to make my earlier reaction seem better than it really was). I got the words out: "I'm sorry. I was wrong. Would you please forgive me?" She nodded and gave me a big hug. Just about the best ten words I ever said.

Since that time, I've tried to accomplish two things: First, don't do things that wound hearts in the first place; and second, if I do, go sort it out with God and my child right away. I don't want my worship to be hindered (see Matthew 5:23-24). I don't want my prayers to be hindered (see Psalm 66:18). And I don't want my relationship with my child to be hindered.

I suspect that you really don't either.

Make a list right now of the things that must be discussed with your children. If they're asleep or not around, pray that God will give you the right words and the earliest opportunity to ask their forgiveness. If they're in the other room, *go get them now* and teach them what only you can teach them. Humble yourself. Go hat in hand to your children, and be forgiven.

Roberto Assagioli said, "Without forgiveness life is governed by . . . an endless cycle of resentment and retaliation." Please kill this cycle, and ask your child's forgiveness.

When Others Offend Us

And what about the other side, when someone has offended us?

Well, there's inaccurate teaching floating around Christian circles on this one. It can be summarized as follows: "If you're a Christian, you have to forgive every-body because you're just a sinner who's been forgiven by God. It doesn't matter what the other person has done, or if he is sorry, or even if he has asked for forgiveness; you must forgive him." Have you heard it expressed something like this? If you teach this to your children, you'll be doing them a great disservice.

It's just plain wrong. God never asks us to do more than He does. In fact, He wants us to be like Him, and to do things *just like* He does. And what does God do in this area? Well, He's *willing* to forgive everybody and always keeps the way open to forgiveness. He works on the sinner to prompt him to seek forgiveness. But He only *forgives* those who ask for forgiveness through the aton-ing work of Jesus, repent of their sins, purpose to obey Him, and make restitution where required.

God *doesn't* forgive everyone. Hell is going to be full of people whom God never forgave because they never listened to His rebuke and sought forgiveness.

And we shouldn't forgive everyone. When they ask our forgiveness, we should forgive them or God won't forgive us (see Matthew 6:14-15; Luke 6:37). But if they never ask, we shouldn't forgive (see John 20:23). We should, like God, always be willing to forgive. And we should pray for the offender so that he'll seek forgive-ness.

Jesus said it clearly: "If your brother sins, *rebuke* him, and if he *repents*, forgive him" (Luke 17:3). If someone has sinned, we should love him enough to go to him with a loving rebuke. If he repents, we should forgive him immediately and gladly. But if he doesn't repent, we shouldn't forgive. He hasn't satisfied the condition nec-essary for forgiveness to take place. Our hearts are kept from bitterness and resentment *if* we will continue to pray for him with sincerity and love until he repents and we can forgive him with rejoicing.

How can this be taught to children? Start with the biblical background, but once again example is the surest way to victory.

Rebuke your children when they sin. Then take the next step: Tell your children to rebuke you respectfully when you sin. And if they do, thank them, ask their forgiveness, and ask them to pray for you.

Pretty powerful teaching on your part, don't you think?

Help them do this with others, including adults, who have sinned against them. And if someone has sinned against you both, with God's help go together and let your children see how to lovingly rebuke a sinning brother with the intent of restoring him. Let them see you forgive a repentant heart. And let them see you maintain your rebuke, with love and grief, in the face of an unrepentant heart.

In other words, let them see you be like God.

___ *Little Samaritans* ___

"But a Samaritan, as he traveled, came where the man was; and when he saw him, he took pity on him" (Luke 10:33).

When we hear the story of the good Samaritan, we usually sit in our seats and smugly judge the priest and the Levite who "passed by on the other side."

And all too often, we can be just like them.

Most people take pity on their own family and close friends. Many people take pity on their neighbors and others who they would consider friends or acquaintances. But few act like this Samaritan. Without fanfare he took pity on a complete stranger. He was a man who poured out his time and money without thought of repayment, and asked no questions at all. He obviously rested in the fact that "a generous man will prosper; he who refreshes others will himself be refreshed" (Proverbs 11:25).

Even as *we* travel along the road of life, we come upon strangers who need our help. It's not enough that our children observe us controlling our tempers at the obstacles in our paths. It's not enough that they notice how well we deal with inconveniences. They must be able to see us help lovingly and cheerfully, or they'll never learn the simple lessons that there *are* no strangers in the believer's life and that a person is your neighbor because God has placed him in your path.

We can too easily fail even in the exact parallel to Jesus' illustration. We travel down the highway, and if we see someone in trouble or injured or with a stalled car, we can "pass by on the other side."

The whole idea of being an ambassador for Christ, of giving selflessly and without expectation of return, of seeing people as Christ sees them rather than as inconveniences, will be lost on our children. By our omission in training we'll be teaching them to be cold, calloused, and aloof.

There's no luck or chance or happenstance in the lives of God's faithful sons and daughters. All things come from the hand of God. Every person in your path was known by God—even *put* there by God—before you were ever born. But today it's not hard to picture someone driving home from a seminar on evangelism and driving right past the soul he's supposed to evangelize.

Of course, we must be prudent. A woman passing three able men on a lonely road at night should still be a good Samaritan. But if her spirit is uncomfortable, she should be a good Samaritan at the next telephone or service station along the road.

Clearly and boldly teach your children to be little Samaritans. Do this by your own example and by watching their walk and instructing them how to help someone who needs them, for no reason other than it's what Jesus Himself would do.

Jesus told the man who prompted this story of faithfulness: "Go and do likewise."
So go and do likewise.

___ *Poor and Broken* ___

Let me say first that I'm not opposed to honest business or financial success, because God isn't opposed to it. Our God is a God of bounty and blessing, and He can pour it upon us with both hands. Scripture is chock-full of statements and examples of material blessing now, here on earth. God's boundaries are that we accept success as a blessing and don't go after it as though it's our god.

I grew up on the philosophy that you were what you made of yourself. If people were down, it was strictly because they were lazy and had too little initiative to pick themselves up "by their own bootstraps" in a country where everyone had the freedom to do it. Anyone can be what they want to be, with a little pluck and luck. I agreed with the man who said that being broke was only temporary, while being poor was a state of mind.

If you've been weaned on the "American Dream" like most American parents, you probably feel pretty much the same way. So what follows may be tough for you to read. It was tough for me to learn. But I encourage you to read it anyway. No one said this was going to be easy.

Discerning the Poor

The Bible doesn't promote laziness. Scripture condemns the sluggard and tells him that poverty will come against him like a bandit or an armed man (see Proverbs 6:11; 24:34). We are told, "If a man will not work, he shall not eat" (2 Thessalonians 3:10), and that we are to be ambitious for a quiet life, minding our own business,

and working with our hands (see 1 Thessalonians 4:11).
Clearly we are to encourage everyone we know to trust
the Lord for the supply of daily needs, and at the same
time to say: "Sow your seed in the morning, and at
evening let not your hands be idle, for you do not know
which will succeed, whether this or that, or whether
both will do equally well" (Ecclesiastes 11:6).

Laziness is a particular problem in a country that has
taught people that they're "deprived" or "underprivi-
leged," and that they're "entitled" to have a certain
share of the pie regardless of what they're willing to do.
We have seen the creation, in some cases, of a "gourmet"
poor who really *are* lazy, demanding, arrogant, judg-
mental, and envious. The sight of people taking handouts
from the government when they are capable of working
must, if Scripture has any meaning, be displeasing to
God.

You have to learn how to discern true poverty from
the "gourmet" variety, and then teach this ability to your
children. And don't go by government statistics that
declare people poor based on some arbitrary salary
level. Take the old-fashioned way and simply find out
who is *really* hurting in spite of their best efforts.

We have to face the plain, scriptural fact that there
were a lot of poor people then, are now, and will be right
up to the Second Coming. Jesus told us this Himself (see
John 12:8). And there are those of us who need to learn
that we have an obligation beyond our words of encouragement to the truly needy (see James 2:15-16).

In fact, we know that it's God who bestows wealth as
He chooses. We are encouraged over and over again to
receive things with contentment, no matter how much
or how little, from the hand of God (see Philippians
4:11-13). No one should dare to claim to be a self-made
man for the simple reason that these are exactly the kind
of men that God unmakes.

And neither are we to sit in judgment or condemnation. Mocking the poor is not popular with our God (see Proverbs 17:5).

Helping the Poor

After clearing out the false ideas about the poor from our own and our children's hearts, we have one simple duty: to help. God has given us a simple truth: "The righteous care about justice for the poor, but the wicked have no such concern" (Proverbs 29:7).

You must teach your children to have a deep concern about justice for the poor. There are plenty of poor right in your own city. You will *not* be living up to the spirit of the verse by sitting around and praying for them if you do nothing else. And sending a check to an organization that helps the poor is good, but it's pretty abstract. If you want your children to truly "lack nothing" (Proverbs 28:27), you must find ways to help the poor which involves you and your kids.

Take the poor food and clothing. Have your plumber fix their pipes or your mechanic fix their cars. Take them to your doctor. Take their kids to tee-ball games. If you're really bold, you can invite God's poor into your home and feed them. But remember that the point is to help the people, not just to discharge a duty or salve a conscience.

One of the activities that has really helped our family is to spend an afternoon at the grocery store buying food for the poor. Then we deliver the food, letting our children see this aspect of God's world up close. By being sensitive to the feelings and dignity of those who we help, we have shown our children how to respect people—no matter their financial status.

Many children in this affluent age stand in great danger of being swallowed up by materialism and by the mistaken belief that this is just how things will always be. It isn't true. Most of the world is poor—dirt poor.

If your children aren't taught how to relate to this *in a personal way*, they'll be living as though they're on another planet, and they'll be of only limited usefulness to God.

Try to get your church involved with your family in helping the poor. And don't limit yourselves to your hometown, either. The world has always been overwhelmingly poor. In most countries, there are the very few rich and the very many poor; often, the very few use their position to grind the very many into the dirt. Take your blinders off and show your children the reality that surrounds them, and then *do* something about it with your children. Our church has had great joy preparing shoe boxes full of clothes, toiletries, books, and toys for the orphans of Uganda.

There is a warning in Scripture: "If a man shuts his ears to the cry of the poor, he too will cry out and not be answered" (Proverbs 21:13). You don't want to cry out and not be answered. You don't want your *children* to cry out and not be answered. The verse is deep theology in the simplest of words: Help, or you won't get any yourself.

Do you realize the importance of helping the poor? Have you gotten this across to your children? Is God looking at you or your children as people who stand pleading before Him while you shut up your ears and look down your nose at the poor? If so, you and your children are in big trouble.

For if God won't listen to you, who will?

Seek to be an excellent example to your children. Frank McKinney Hubbard said, "The reason parents no longer lead their children in the right direction is because the parents aren't going that way themselves." Don't let this be true of you.

Part 2

Six Crucial Ingredients

5

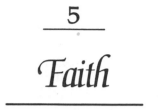

Faith

Fiction: Even faith has its limitations in a fallen world; you have to be realistic.

Fact: This is the victory that has overcome the world, even our faith (1 John 5:4).

Faith is essential.

The Lord God Almighty has chosen to base His dealings with all people, including children, on the principle of faith alone. No matter who wants to approach Him, he *must* approach with faith if he wants to receive anything. God says to us:

- "Without faith it is impossible to please God, because anyone who comes to him must believe that he exists and that he rewards those who *earnestly* seek him" (Hebrews 11:6).

- "If you do not stand firm in your faith, you will not stand *at all*" (Isaiah 7:9).

- To the *faithful* God shows Himself faithful (see Psalm 18:25).

God wants you and your children to believe Him. And He wants you to believe Him all of the time—whether or not you feel like it or understand or agree. And as a parent you *must* be faithful, not just for you, but also for your children. One of the awesome truths of Scripture is that your children can suffer for *your* unfaithfulness (see Numbers 14:33).

When Jesus told Peter to drop the nets for a catch, Peter's mind, loaded with logic and experience, resisted. But his heart believed: "Because you say so, I will let down the nets" (Luke 5:5). This simple act led to the Lord's miraculous response and changed Peter's entire life, as he "left everything and followed him" (verse 11).

___ *Walking by Faith* ___

Many of us have realized we can't work our way into heaven. We've accepted God's Word that we can be saved from the awful penalty of our sins through faith in the atoning work of Jesus on the cross. And we are sure that our faith in this act guarantees our salvation from the hideous presence of sin when we go to be with Jesus Every child must be exposed to these fundamental beliefs early and often, and encouraged to commit his heart, without restraint.

But why do we stop there? Where is our reckless belief in *all* of God's promises? Why do we try to live our new life by a different principle from the one that *gave* us new life? Why don't we teach our children that faith is the key for *this* life, as well as for eternity? Why don't we show our children by our own prayers that we pray for even very little things, and that God is bothered by our praying when we *don't* bother Him with our praying?

The reason is simple: We are not "certain of what we do not see" (Hebrews 11:1). We are like the Galatians who saw faith not as a life principle, but rather as a ticket to get into the arena of good works. They got saved by faith but were going to walk the Christian walk by their own strength. Paul was merciless on them—and us: "Are you so foolish? After beginning with the Spirit, are you now trying to attain your goal by human effort?   How is it that you are turning back to those weak and miserable principles?" (Galatians 3:3; 4:9).

Amen!

We must teach our children to believe *all* of God's promises, including:

- Salvation by faith from the *power* of sin. We don't have to give in to temptations, or to the world that finds such a willing partner in the flesh, or to re-enslavement to our earlier bondage. We are "more than conquerors" (Romans 8:37).

- Salvation by faith from the *plague* of sin. We don't have to give in to fear, worry, anxiety, confusion, pain, sickness, fear of dying "before our time," dissatisfaction with work, or concerns about material needs. God is gracious and compassionate, waiting to fill to overflowing those who seek Him by faith and persevere in this faith: "Whatever you ask for in prayer, believe [present tense] that you have received it [past tense], and it *will* be yours [future tense]" (Mark 11:24). This doesn't mean that you won't have any troubles, or that you're guaranteed health and wealth. But it *does* mean that God cares deeply about your welfare. What audacity to think He's a grudging Father!

- Salvation by faith from the *purpose* of sin. Before you're a believer you *have* to sin; it's your nature. You're part of Satan's master plan. But after salvation, you are "God's workmanship, created in Christ Jesus to do good works" (Ephesians 2:10), by *His* strength.

Faith is the key to victory right here and now from the penalty, power, plague, and purpose of sin, and someday from the very presence of sin. Pretty simple, isn't it? Does God mean that you just believe Him and He responds? You bet He does. You can take it to the bank before you actually have it in your hand, because He says so.

In Action

Our children must learn God's Word, including His promises and the faith that guarantees their delivery. But these young ones will be poorly taught unless they see evidence of walking by faith in their parents and spiritual family. Only by observing faith in action can their head knowledge of faith ever become heart knowledge. And remember, mental agreement is not faith. Your children need to see biblical hero-type faith in action in you. "I will show you my faith," James says, "by what I do" (James 2:18).

A few years ago, the Lord prompted me to run for state representative against an unopposed, three-term incumbent who was anti-God, anti-life, and pro-sex education down to the kindergarten level. Although I could see the value of running, a big part of me said I didn't have the time or energy. But I chose to do it, because it was the right thing to do.

It was one of the most challenging times of my life. I got very little sleep and felt like I never had a moment of rest. I also had a bladder infection and spent much of my door-to-door time with a fever. I would walk up to a door, wipe off my forehead, comb my hair, and then try to smile as I shared my views. I had people curse me at their front door because of my biblically based stands on issues.

And I "lost" the election. All of that effort, and the other guy got more votes. But I had purposed in my heart from the beginning that I was going to run for God and truth, and not for an office. He honored that commitment.

I got to share my message in some amazing places. The local newspaper sent me a questionnaire, which included the question: "In ten words or less, tell us what you believe to be the greatest danger facing our state in the next five years." I wrestled with God for days before I finally put down the answer He had put in my heart: "Given the incredible moral decline, probably the wrath of God." Not smart politics, perhaps, but that answer put me and my message on page one.

I didn't *feel* like a hero. I felt like somebody slugging it out with an ugly, unseen enemy. I didn't know if I was going to make it through some days. But that wasn't how my children viewed it. They were totally supportive and appreciative. Laura and Peter told me that they weren't sure they wanted me to win because it would mean I would have to spend more time away from home, but they sure thought it was great to attack the enemy's strongholds and deliver uncompromised truth. Perhaps the best results of that step of faith took place in my own home.

Many Christians refuse to believe and act until they've got all the details worked out in their heads. Folks, this is *sight*, not faith. Let your children see your confidence that God will give you fuller understanding later. As Augustine said, "Understanding is the reward of faith. Therefore seek not to understand that you may believe, but believe that you may understand."

Faith doesn't mean having a frontal lobotomy. The person of faith faces his fears and doubts, and even the gloomy facts about the situation, and says, "They're all there, but they just don't matter."

There's a story of a church in a farm community where a drought had been raging for many months. A prayer meeting was called to ask the Lord for blessing in the form of rain. As the leader stood up, he looked around at the congregation and asked: "Brothers and sisters, if you're here to pray for rain, *where are your umbrellas?*"

Believing always involves attentiveness *and* responsiveness to God. Jesus asked, "Why do you call me, 'Lord, Lord,' and do not do what I say?" (Luke 6:46). Your action should always be based on your faith and must always work with your faith. God doesn't want you to act *instead* of believing; He wants you to act *because* you believe.

Not in Fear

Faith can conquer fears in your children, including the little ones. Don't try to act as if you don't have any fears; you won't be able to help your kids if they think they've got a problem you can't understand. Admit to them that you have fears, but tell them how your faith in your Papa-God keeps you from giving in to these fears. Tell them that with Jesus there's *nothing* to fear. Answer a fear of the dark with a ringing description of the angels that are there to serve and protect them (see Hebrews 1:14). The *only* answer to fear is faith.

Faith doesn't mean having a frontal lobotomy. The person of faith faces his fears and doubts, and even the gloomy facts about the situation, and says, "They're all there, but they just don't matter." We can be like our spiritual father, Abraham:

> He is our father in the sight of God, in whom he believed—the God who gives life to the dead and calls things that are not as though they were. Against all hope, Abraham in hope believed.... Without weakening in his faith, he faced the fact that his body was as good as dead—since he was about a hundred years old—and that Sarah's womb was also dead. *Yet he did not waiver through unbelief* regarding the promise of God, but was strengthened in his faith and gave glory to God, being fully persuaded that God had power to do what he had promised (Romans 4:17-21).

Faith can move mountains! It's bigger than everything you can see because it taps into a world of invisible majesty that dwarfs the things that surround us. You find out about this powerful, invisible world by knowing the clear written Word that God has so graciously given us.

Learn the Word. Understand it and believe it—it *belongs* to you. It's part of your inheritance as an adopted son of God (see Deuteronomy 4:6-8). Don't let anyone cheat you out of its fullness.

Teach your young ones to move the newly discovered promises into their hearts, whether or not the words seem logical, or "feel right," or match the experience of most of the world. As they begin this true walk of faith on the true path of power, you should also teach them to remember this: "Everyone who wants to live a godly life in Christ Jesus will be persecuted" (2 Timothy 3:12). They'll need to know this when a faithless world—and maybe a faithless church—opposes them.

And one more thing ought to be kept in mind.

Don't forget your umbrella.

___ I *Know* a *Person Who* . . . ___

"We live by faith, not by sight" (2 Corinthians 5:7).

As soon as you learn and come to believe this great truth, and teach your children to do the same, you'll make an interesting discovery: This verse doesn't represent the experience of many Christians.

The problem, of course, is that the vast majority has had more experience living by sight than by faith. We teach our children to live by the details of "the faith," but not how to simply *live* by faith. Once you and your children start to grasp the meaning of this "faith" business, you and they will begin to encounter responses that will have a common theme: "But I know a person who . . ."

A person who what?

- A person who asked to be rescued and wasn't and had to learn "why God allowed this to happen to him."

- A person who asked for protection but only got God's consolation in the terrible problems that followed.

- A person who asked God to be with him during a period of great trouble and got hard lessons in the "valley of the shadow of death" instead.

- A person who asked to be delivered from some terrible onslaught but received only the grace to deal with the disaster.

- A person who prayed but got no answer.

But Scripture declares: "Let God be true, and every man a liar" (Romans 3:4).

No matter what the situation, there's someone who knows someone who didn't receive what they supposedly sought by faith.

God is a loving and protective Father who guards our lives and keeps us from unnecessary suffering. He's also a God who calls us to follow Him regardless of the cost, and a God who may call us to undergo some temporary pain to further His plan, bringing Him glory and us maturity, joy, and rewards (see James 1:2-4).

Too often we preach faith, but live by experience. And as a Christian community, we are living with the consequences of this sad state.

In every case of "I know a person who...," you'll be assured that the person used in the example is a Christian. Sometimes, to emphasize the point, you'll be advised that the person was a strong Christian. The evidence seems overwhelming. What can you or your children possibly say?

You can say this: "We live by faith, not by sight." You can, and should, look at Scripture with your children and these people. One thing you'll find there is an answer to the "I know a person who..."

"Because he loves me," says the LORD, "I *will* rescue him; I *will* protect him, for he acknowledges my name. He will call upon me, and I *will* answer him; I *will* be with him in trouble, I *will* deliver him and honor him. With long life *will* I satisfy him and show him my salvation" (Psalm 91:14-16).

And when God says, "I will," He means it. The cardinal truth that you must teach your children is that they should judge all experience (sight) by the Word of God and that they should *never* judge the Word of God by anyone's experience. Don't ever be discouraged by the huge quantity of "I know a person who . . ." examples that supposedly undermine what you know to be true from Scripture. Sight is always easier and more appealing to the flesh than faith.

Just remember that truth is truth—even if no one believes it.

The Only Thing That Counts

If someone you had confidence in told you that they knew the *only* thing that counts, you would surely want to know this thing and share it with your children. Many of us are looking for such a key to knowledge. We would like to know God's first priority, the number one item on His agenda. To say with confidence, "I know the only thing that counts," would give clarity to our hearts and minds and direction to our actions.

Has God given us this information?

Scripture says, with incredible directness and simplicity: "The only thing that counts is faith expressing itself through love" (Galatians 5:6). Period. Faith is the primary thing, love is the vehicle, and God is our authority. It's as simple a statement as can be found in Scripture. Believe it.

You may have been concerned that *love* was not listed as one of the six crucial ingredients of proactive parenting. But love is part and parcel of faith, the first of these

six ingredients. Love—for God, His Word, other people—
is the mouthpiece of faith.

There is no living faith without love. John reminds
us, "We know that we have passed from death to life,
because we love our brothers" (1 John 3:14). The two are
forever intertwined: "And this is his command: to
believe in the name of his Son, Jesus Christ, and to *love*
one another as he commanded us" (1 John 3:23). Faith
without love for God and our brothers and sisters in
Christ is dead, cold, unbiblical, and impossible.

And there is no true love without faith. John says, "If
anyone obeys his word, God's love is truly made complete in him. This is how we know we are in him: Whoever
claims to live in him must walk as Jesus did" (1 John
2:5-6). Obedience to the Word comes through faith, and
it's the only way to let God's love fill us. No eternally
intimate and holy relationship between people is possible without faith in God at the center of it. Love without
faith is pointless, powerless, unbiblical, and impossible.

Don't just teach your children to believe, teach them
to love. Don't just encourage your children to be kind
to others, teach them to believe God, which releases
the floodgates that will allow them to love God and
the family of God and to lay down their lives for their
brothers.

It's so important that I'll say it one more time: "The
only thing that counts is faith expressing itself through
love."

Sounds like a motto for a homemade plaque, doesn't
it?

I suggest putting it on the wall, right by the front
door.

6

Integrity

Fiction: It can be difficult to decide how to apply Scripture.

Fact: How long will you waver between two opinions? If the LORD is God, follow him; but if Baal is God, follow him (1 Kings 18:21).

Thoreau said it well: "As for conforming outwardly, and living your own life inwardly, I do not think much of that."

Me, neither.

We live today in a large compartment complex. We have our work compartment, our church compartment, our family compartment. And we have our own little compartment where we hide. Sometimes the differences between these compartments are great; other times they are more subtle.

Integrity is oneness and wholeness, a deep consistency of life and thought. It's a moral soundness that gives its possessor an accurate guide so that he can and will walk with conviction, purpose, and security. Only men and women of integrity can be carefree, not worried about what they said to whom or who will find them out.

Ralph Waldo Emerson described well the man of integrity:

> He conquers, because his arrival alters the face
> of affairs ... appointed by Almighty God to stand

for a fact—invincibly persuaded of that fact in himself—so that the most confident and the most violent persons learn that here is resistance on which both impudence and terror are wasted.... Men of character are the conscience of the society to which they belong.

A person of integrity clings to moral consistency as though it's a life preserver. He guards his reputation with diligence and vigilance and is relentlessly honest, conducting his affairs with justice (see Psalm 112:5). He knows that "a trustworthy man keeps a secret" (Proverbs 11:13).

And he knows how critical this virtue is to the development of his children. He'll go out of his way to live this out in front of them and, without pride, to drive this home to them. He'll openly disagree with a compliment about him he knows to be only partly true, and he'll stand his ground in a discussion when he's outnumbered ten to one.

And what of the opposite of a man of integrity? A double-minded man. He's a chameleon, changing his colors to fit his surroundings. You never know where he really stands, what he's really thinking, or how he really feels about God or you—or maybe anything. The only thing worse than dealing with a double-minded man is to *be* a double-minded man or woman.

But *you* can be a man or woman of integrity.

Ask God to give you an undivided heart. Ask Him to help you resist the many temptations to compartmentalize your life, and instead make your life a beacon that will shine right through the worldly fog. Ask God to help you as a parent not to waver back and forth between being too unavailable or tough on the one hand, and caving in and making too many promises or being too soft on the other.

God will assign to you, as a person of integrity, more responsibility, greater trust, and richer blessings. You can be like the man to whom Nehemiah assigned responsibility for Jerusalem, "because he was a man of integrity and feared God more than most men do" (Nehemiah 7:2).

___ *Dealing with Contradictions* ___

Our integrity starts with the understanding that we have a God of integrity who has given us the Bible—a book we can use with complete and total confidence in its message.

I want to make something perfectly clear: Every word of God is utterly flawless (see Proverbs 30:5), and there is not a single contradiction in the Bible.

How do I know this? I don't; I *believe* it. God says that His Word is firm and reliable. If you accept in your heart and mind that God's Word contains even the *hint* of a contradiction, you strip yourself of any chance to experience the full power of God's might in your life. And you will have undercut your own integrity.

You are made up of spirit and body. Your spirit consists of your heart, the seat of love; your mind, which understands the things taught by the spirit; and your will, the very essence of your spirit, which chooses to believe or not believe the things perceived by heart and mind. Your body is your physical makeup, including your brain.

Your brain and your mind are *not* the same thing. You relate to many things through your senses and their interpreter, the brain. But the brain is part of fallen flesh, and your understanding can't stop there. Ideas must move as quickly as possible from your brain to your mind.

We are encouraged in Scripture to trust in God and not to lean on our own fleshly understanding (see Proverbs

3:5). We are also told that "we have the mind of Christ" (1 Corinthians 2:16). Too many Christians end their study of Scripture in their brains, and so the words are just words to them, compelling them to no action, leaving them with the empty feeling that there's nothing there for them.

"But we have the mind of Christ" and can go on to believe and obey the Word, which will *lead* to understanding (see Psalm 111:10).

Teach your children first to approach the Bible with the confidence that God's Word is 100 percent correct, that He is only telling them one story, and that absolute truth is indivisible and unchangeable and doesn't come in plaids. They must be taught to believe this in their hearts and minds, and not in their brains. The brain works on reason alone and *looks* for contradictions. Reason alone will never understand what only faith can deliver.

Then, teach them about an interesting phenomenon: Some of the most exciting insights in Scripture are found in the apparent contradictions. God loves to hide His truth so that only His faithful ones can find it: "It is the glory of God to conceal a matter; to search out a matter is the glory of kings" (Proverbs 25:2).

This makes apparent contradictions exciting because there's something very special there. Your children need to be excited when they come across these things. They will be, if you are and if they understand that it's their *brains* that are fuzzy, not the Bible. They can begin a study, perhaps with you, that will lead them to magnificent truth (see Psalm 27:7-8).

As Kin Hubbard said, "T'ain't what a man don't know that hurts him; it's what he knows that just ain't so."

And as far as the Word of God is concerned, there just ain't no contradictions.

__ *Following Through* __

I don't think most of us have a very clear idea of just how rebellious and disobedient God's own sons and daughters can be. Today, most Christians wouldn't even *consider* obeying God on something that sounded strange to them or that required some cost or inconvenience or change of lifestyle.

Where is the uncompromising and unyielding *commitment* to the Lord and His Word, no matter the cost? Where are those who *submit* to God's authority, whether the command is "appealing" or not? And where is the simple, day-to-day *obedience* to the Word of God in *all* of its particulars, wherever that may lead?

They just aren't there.

Commitment, submission, and obedience have almost become a joke; only God isn't laughing and the joke is on us. We are raising a new generation in a lawless culture, in a lawless religion, and more often than not, in a lawless family. How do we expect kids to be young men and women of godly character when they don't even know how to obey? It would be funny if it weren't so sad.

Following through involves obedience to God and His Word. Alignment with the Word is a matching up with God's perfection and is the basis for being a person of integrity.

We need to teach our children how to follow through on what God is telling them to do and to hang the cost. First, they have to be taught to commit themselves totally and without reservation to the Lord. Second, they have to be taught to be submissive—gentle, humble, sensitive, and everything else that implies. Third, they need to be taught to be relentlessly obedient—to the point of death if necessary. You must be their example.

And I am talking about *active* obedience, not lip service to God or His Word. Jesus told a parable that is very
instructive here:

> "What do you think? There was a man who had
> two sons. He went to the first and said, 'Son, go and
> work today in the vineyard.' 'I will not,' he answered,
> but later he changed his mind and went. Then the
> father went to the other son and said the same
> thing. He answered, 'I will, sir,' but he did not go.
> Which of the two did what his father wanted?"
> "The first," they answered (Matthew 21:28-31).

Immediate obedience to God is, of course, the highest kind and one likeliest to reap rich blessings. But Jesus
recognizes that some things might not "sound right" to
us at first hearing. There's no severe penalty for taking
the time to think about it, even after your initial reaction
to say no, as long as the next step is obedience. But if
your immediate response is yes, there is a penalty if you
reconsider your decision and disobey. You get no credit
for saying the right *words*; to God, it's the actual obedience or disobedience that's the issue.

If we have taught our children well—primarily by
our example—we should see them becoming committed,
submissive young people who are more and more instantly obedient to God and to you. But give them a little
time, too. Even if their initial reaction is negative, according to Jesus' parable, they haven't actually disobeyed
yet. Give them some time (and perhaps some Scripture)
to consider their attitude and decision. If they obey, no
matter how great their internal struggle, count it as obedience.

Don't fall easy prey to a quick yes that has no sub-
stance to it. If they tell you they'll do it, and don't do it
in a reasonable amount of time, then it's safe to assume
that what you've got is basic disobedience. They get no

points for good intentions. In some ways this is worse than an outright refusal to obey, since it adds lying to rebellion. You need to clean up this act quickly.

Once you've taught your children to follow through—to be committed, submissive, and obedient in their actions—you've got one big danger. What authority will you allow over them in different situations? As they grow, children can learn that their obedience must be prioritized. But when they're young, this is hard for them to perceive. A wise parent will emphasize obedience to God first and to men second, and to men not at all if they stand against God. But beyond that, a parent must guard against ungodly authority taking advantage of his child's innocence and trained obedience in the first place.

If you train your children to follow through, they'll stand tall in the Lord's eyes, "For the eyes of the LORD range throughout the earth to strengthen those whose hearts are fully committed to him" (2 Chronicles 16:9). *Fully* committed like Jesus, who "humbled himself and became obedient to death—even death on a cross!" (Philippians 2:8).

Now *that's* following through.

'Following Through — for You, Too —

Following through involves active commitment, submission, and obedience to God and His Word. Alignment with the Word is a matching up with God's perfection and is the basis for being a person of integrity.

God has His part in the process. When God speaks, He follows through with blessings for obedience and punishments for disobedience. And guess what? You should do the same.

Follow Through on Promises

Dad, you make a promise to take your son to the park on Saturday. It's Saturday, and you're bone-tired. All you want to do is settle in a comfortable place and be left alone. And here comes little Alfred, who can't remember an order for 22 seconds, but is a regular computer bank when it comes to your promises. He says, simply, "Dad, I'm ready to go to the park."

Dad, whether you know it or not, you're at a major crossroad. What you do in the next 60 seconds is going to speak volumes about the value of your word. You basically have four choices.

Saying, "No, I don't think I can," and sticking with it is the worst choice; it teaches Alfred that integrity and your word don't mean much. Saying, "No, I don't think I can," and then changing your mind fairly quickly isn't the best choice, but it shows him you will follow through, given some time to think about it. Saying, "Yes, I'll take you, because it's important to fulfill my word, even though I don't feel like it," is a good choice; you're following through and letting Alfred know that you *have* to do this even when you *don't* feel like it. And finally, saying, "Yes, I'll take you, because I love you and delight in keeping my word," is the best choice—for obvious reasons.

Follow Through on Discipline

The principle of following through also applies to discipline.

Children are action-oriented. They pay a lot more attention to what you do than what you say. "A servant cannot be corrected by mere words; though he understands, he will not respond" (Proverbs 29:19).

Although you might consider tongue-lashings sufficient punishment for any offense, your children may not be so easily intimidated. You may even find that they do things to egg you on so they can see you blow up. Tongue-lashings are no lashings at all. They might humiliate or embarrass your children, or make them bitter or angry, or even destroy their feelings about you and themselves. But mere words cannot make them respond. Nothing is as weightless as a threat allowed to float away on the breeze of inaction (see Ecclesiastes 6:11).

One of the really terrible things about mere words is they are multiplied just like a fool's (see Ecclesiastes 10:14). It's no coincidence that some of the worst-behaved children belong to some of the most verbally obtuse and inactive parents. The more wordy the parents become, the more the children learn to disrespect authority, to *ignore* authority, and to be fundamentally disobedient. In other words, this approach produces just the *opposite* of what is being demanded.

So save the lectures. Instead, give them something to get their attention, cooperation, and remembrance.

Give them action.

Whether it's a spanking, time in, time-out, loss of privileges, or whatever, it's what they need, and perhaps even want. Make sure your children know that one time is all they're going to hear something before they see a blur of action. Some of the saddest words parents ever utter are, "I'm going to tell you just one more time. . . ."

If you combine action and words, you'll not only get obedient children, you'll get peace and delight. Proverbs 29 also says: "The rod of correction imparts wisdom, but a child left to himself disgraces his mother. . . . Discipline your son, and he will give you peace; he will bring delight to your soul" (verses 15 and 17).

Loving your children and sharing enjoyable experiences with them can give you fun and pleasure, but the surest way to peace and delight is for you to use the rod of correction and discipline them. Tell them something

once, expect prompt obedience, and then "hit the beach."
If you still feel helpless and that you just *have* to tell your
kids to do something ten times, do yourself a favor and
reread this section.

Just one more time.

___ O *Promise Me* ___

Most parents like to say that they're men and women
of their word; and yet, they are often lax and tolerant in
expecting the same from their children. You're doing
your child no favors with this approach.

When your child gives his word to anyone on anything, you should insist that he keep it. This isn't optional. Even if it hurts to do it right now, in the end he
will be blessed by God for it. This is the meaning of the
Scripture: "Lord, who may dwell in your sanctuary?
Who may live on your holy hill? He . . . who keeps his
oath even when it hurts. . . . He who does these things
will never be shaken" (Psalm 15:1,4-5).

Seven-year-old Maggie learned this lesson when she
told her little brother John that he could have anything
he wanted out of her toy box, from which she thought
she had removed all the good toys. Well, she had missed
something of great value to her, and of course that's what
he found and wanted. Maggie did not want to keep her
word, and she gave her brother a very hard time. Her
father directed her to return the item as well as to ask
John's forgiveness.

My concern is that most parents would have negoti-
ated and reasoned with their son on the basis that their
daughter had made an "honest" mistake, rather than
insisting on her being a girl of her word. This would
have been a great mistake. They would have missed
teaching her two valuable lessons: to not give her word
without thought and to keep her word—period.

Look for opportunities for your child to make commitments to you and then keep them. This is true training in righteousness. If he wants to do something, say yes if you can; but if there's a logical thing that he should do after that, make him agree to it in advance.

If he wants to go outside in the mud, fine; but he must commit to clean up the mess (or at least help if he's too little to do it all by himself). If he wants to go somewhere, all right; but get a commitment from him on the time by which he'll be back. In short, rather than just giving orders after the fact, get him to agree before the fact to be *responsible*.

Then make him live up to his commitment. He might have agreed rashly to it, but it doesn't make any difference. If he doesn't do it, or does it slowly or grumbling, he should suffer the loss of the privilege the next time and get any other penalties that are appropriate to his disobedience or attitude.

This will teach him responsibility, improve his attitude, improve *your* attitude, and make him speak more thoughtfully. When a child is old enough to understand what he wants, he's old enough to understand what *you* want.

One final thought shouldn't really be necessary to express, but observation says that it is. None of this will work long-term unless you're a person of your word: to employers, to family, to friends, to enemies, to your spouse, to your children. When you make promises, you *must* fulfill them, even if it hurts.

No, *especially* if it hurts.

___ *You Scratch My Back* . . . ___

"The devil is compromise."

Although these are Henrik Ibsen's words and not those of the Bible, they couldn't be more true. *Compromise* is a word that should connote evil to you. It should make you shiver when you hear it. The fact that politicians call politics the "art of compromise" alone ought to be enough to make you drive the word from your vocabulary.

Everything in the world around you and your child reeks of compromise. The majority of books, movies, television, radio, music, and art teach that there are no absolutes, that you have to be pragmatic, that you can't be steadfast in anything and still expect to get ahead—or even get along. The pressure will come to bear on you to compromise on biblical truth, to "be reasonable" in your parenting, and to understand that "rigid" principles just won't work in our modern world.

And then the pressure will move to your children. Peer pressure is a pure pressure to compromise. Satan uses your children's natural desire to be liked against them and encourages them to give up what they know to be right to preserve their "reputation."

Your children can all too easily become like the Jewish leaders who "believed in him. But because of the Pharisees they would not confess their faith for fear they would be put out of the synagogue; for they loved praise from men more than praise from God" (John 12:42-43).

Constantly remind them of Jesus' warning: "Whoever acknowledges me before men, I will also acknowledge him before my Father in heaven. But whoever disowns me before men, I will disown him before my Father in heaven" (Matthew 10:32-33).

Even though my wife and I got a late start on building the principle of no compromise firmly and clearly into our oldest daughter, God has been gracious in allowing our efforts to bear much fruit in her life (see Isaiah 26:12). We taught Laura to run with the Lord and not with the crowd. We explained that yielding on what she knew to be true would tear up her heart. We showed her that the trade of her principles and clear conscience for a bit of shallow "acceptance" was a pretty lousy deal. And we mentioned that boys might offer a poor exchange of a little attention for . . . other things.

At the same time, we tried to get across that neither we nor God were ready for her to become proud, conceited, arrogant, or standoffish. We still wanted her to be involved with the people around her. We wanted her to be gracious in her attitudes and in her words. We wanted her to impact lives—but on God's terms, not her peers'.

And she did. And many times that meant she stood alone. She missed "social opportunities" and faced strong rejection from her peers. There were times of real loneliness as she refused to compromise on her principles just to be popular. And though we can know in our hearts that we're right before God, it's still tough to feel like an outcast a good part of the time.

But do you know what happened? Laura graduated as valedictorian of her class. She also won the "Davis Award," given by a vote of teachers and students to the graduate who most exemplified Christian character. And she was crowned homecoming queen.

While not everyone will win awards and honors, this experience does show that someone can stand on biblical principles, refuse to compromise, and still be gentle (see 2 Timothy 2:23-26) and honored by at least some people—and always by God.

Integrity should mean for your kids that they're people who maintain their principles no matter what crowd they're in. It should mean that they remain true to their Lord no matter what pressure or trouble comes. And it should mean that they're the same over time, just as their God is (see Malachi 3:6; James 1:17).

And integrity means knowing with conviction that ultimately there are no gray areas except in our own fuzzy minds and hearts. We have a black-and-white God, with black-and-white principles, who will at the end bless or curse people in a very memorable, black-and-white way. We need to be crystal-clear, black-and-white followers of God and show our children how to be the same.

No compromise.

Tattletales and
___ *Other Stories* ___

What's our reaction when we hear about a public official who "blows the whistle" on dishonesty in government? Or a person who walks away from a conspiracy and turns in the criminals? Or a person who was told to be dishonest on the job but goes to his boss' superiors instead?

Our reaction is not, "What a disgusting tattletale!" We appreciate the courage and integrity that the person is showing to the world. If the person suffers for his honesty, we become outraged and demand justice. When the guilty are brought to justice, we whoop it up.

But then our children come to us in exactly the same way, with possible truth about a certain situation, and our reaction becomes fuzzy and unprincipled and, all too often, wrong. We chastise children who bring us the truth and warn them sternly not to be so low as to "snitch" on their peers, who may be exercising criminal behavior toward them or someone else.

Well, these children will learn the lesson. Far be it from them to ever tell *you* the truth again.

God *delights* in integrity and those who have it. He wants parents to encourage both an appreciation for the truth and the telling of that truth. The false code of honor, which says that you should never say a skunk stinks, is totally bogus and destined to aid evil in running amok.

Obviously, children lie sometimes, and their motives are not always pure. So how does a parent encourage integrity without encouraging lying, gossip, rumor, slander, and slur?

You must first *teach your children to love decency and truth.* If they don't know what's right or wrong, or don't love the right and hate the wrong, you can skip the rest of this section until a later time.

If they see something wrong, *they should follow biblical principles of correction.* They should be taught to go first to the offender alone before getting you or anyone else involved. If the other child refuses to listen to the child of integrity, and continues in his bad ways, then it's proper to get you involved.

You should demand truth, even if it implicates the one telling it, and should severely punish any lying. All lying is bad, but lying to get another child into trouble is particularly rotten. The scriptural punishment for perjury was simple: The perjurer got the punishment that the other person would have gotten if the story were true (see Deuteronomy 19:16-21). Perjury will disappear pretty quickly and permanently if you adopt this practice.

Make sure that the truth-teller is careful in his choice of words. Let him know that you won't listen to gossip or slander and that a self-righteous attitude is unacceptable.

Motives are important. Watch how the truth-teller reacts to the punishment of the wrongdoer. If he seems to enjoy it, be like God and stop the punishment (see Proverbs 24:17-18). Then have a little chat with the almost child of integrity. Explain mercy to him. Give him an example of mercy by not punishing him for his rejoicing over the problems of another—this time.

If the truth has been told and the motives are right, then you should *praise the truth-teller.* Then he'll know that virtue is commendable.

Do you ever wonder why honesty can be so scarce among children? Perhaps it's because adults often aren't honest or don't teach their children about honesty and its value. Or maybe it's just because we don't use the obvious opportunities to teach it.

Be a parent who uses opportunities—and uses them wisely. Show your children what the Bible has to say about a person of integrity. And then teach them to live a life of integrity—by living one yourself.

7

Holiness

Fiction: Asking people to obey all of God's Word is legalistic and unreasonable. We live in an age of grace.

Fact: But just as he who called you is holy, so be holy in all you do; for it is written, "Be holy, because I am holy" (1 Peter 1:15-16).

Is it possible, in the midst of an evil age, to live a holy life?
Yes.

Holiness is not only possible—it's *mandatory*. The real question is: Is it possible to truly live life if it isn't holy?
No.

__ *Set Apart* __

God wants you—*all* of you. Every niche, every nook, every cranny. You don't serve fine meals on dirty dishes or refreshments in spotted glasses. God doesn't either. He isn't going to take His joyful and powerful message of hope and love and serve it to the world in a dirty vessel. He never has, and He isn't going to start with you.

We have been made holy by God: "For he chose us in him before the creation of the world to be holy and blameless in his sight" (Ephesians 1:4). If we or our children know Christ Jesus as personal Savior, *we already are holy.* We have "become the righteousness of God" (2 Corinthians 5:21). We have a "new self, created to be like God in true righteousness and holiness" (Ephesians 4:24).

But unfortunately, we don't have to live up to what we already are. We still have free will, and we can choose to be, for the flimsiest of pleasures, a friend of the world. "You adulterous people, don't you know that friendship with the world is hatred toward God? Anyone who *chooses* to be a friend of the world becomes an enemy of God" (James 4:4).

Whose friend are you?

God's High Standards

Holiness isn't optional for a believer. By walking in faith and obedience to God's Word through the power of the Holy Spirit, we can, without a doubt, walk a holy walk on a minute-by-minute basis. If we couldn't walk a holy walk, why would God tell us "to be holy in all you do" (1 Peter 1:15), or to "be perfect, therefore, as your heavenly Father is perfect" (Matthew 5:48)? He tells us these things because He means them.

"To fear the LORD is to hate evil" (Proverbs 8:13). To hate evil—not just avoid it, not just resist it, but *hate* it because we serve a holy and awesome God! Fearing the Lord is the beginning of wisdom: "But the wisdom that comes from heaven is *first of all* pure" (James 3:17).

Walking in Holiness

Are there steps to walking in holiness?

Controlling your tongue (see James 3:2) leads to holiness, with particular emphasis on doing "everything without complaining or arguing, so that you may become blameless and pure" (Philippians 2:14). And with thoughts and words in check, you can be "clear minded and self-controlled so that you can pray" (1 Peter 4:7).

But isn't this tough? How do we do it?

His divine power has given us everything we need for life and godliness through our knowledge of him who called us by his own glory and goodness. Through these he has given us his very great and precious promises, so that through them you may participate in the divine nature and escape the corruption in the world caused by evil desires (2 Peter 1:3-4).

Does God really expect this much from us? Aren't we in the "age of grace"? These very questions show how little we understand the true depth and meaning of biblical grace. Paul knew the depth of this grace and what it meant in all its fullness. Paul told Titus, his "true son in the faith," that grace is much more than God's forgiving us when we do fall. Grace, in fact, is the very thing that can keep us from falling in the first place— *if* we will learn what it's trying to teach us (see Titus 2:11-14).

God wants you—all of you. Every niche,
every nook, every cranny.

You *can* keep from falling by an absolute reliance on the power of God—for every breath, every decision, every step, every minute. If you believe that He's given you this power, it's enough. It's sufficient. In fact, it's all there is. It's the grace itself that finally gives us the ability to fully obey God's law (see Romans 8:3b-4).

Can parents today teach their children how to walk as holy as they already are in God's sight? We can, absolutely. We can hold God's standards high, fill our children with the purifying Word, teach them and show them how to control their tongues, and work with them on self-control by the power of God. We can protect them from much and prepare them for the rest.

__ *Inside Out* __

One of the biggest problems that any parent has is how to *internalize* his values into the spirits of his children.

This is difficult, and many parents don't even know that it needs to be done. Instead, they *impose* their values onto the spirits of their children, often producing the appearance of obedience and control while they graciously accept the applause of their admiring friends.

It looks good right up to the time the lid blows off.

An excellent scriptural example of the difference between internalizing and imposing is found in 2 Chronicles 23–24. Joash is made king of Judah at the age of seven, largely because of the efforts of the chief priest, Jehoiada. Jehoiada, a godly man, removes the boy's wicked grandmother, who had tried to kill the boy, and places Joash on the throne of David. Jehoiada not only made many important decisions for the new king, but also helped him in his decision making. The only thing the priest forgot to do was to internalize God's values into the boy king. "Joash did what was right in the eyes of the LORD *all the years of Jehoiada the priest*" (24:2).

This is equivalent to someone saying about your child, "He did what was right in the eyes of the Lord all the years of his parents." Do you really think that's enough?

It wasn't enough for Joash. As soon as Jehoiada was dead, Joash went completely out of control. He listened to phony praise and took the advice of false counselors. He abandoned the very temple that he had helped to restore with Jehoiada and went on to worship Asherah poles and idols. Finally, he had the son of Jehoiada put to death. He "did not remember the kindness Zechariah's father Jehoiada had shown him but killed his son" (24:22). Joash paid the price when those who were offended by this incredible ungratefulness killed him in his bed.

Instilling God's Values

There's no question that it takes more wisdom and time to internalize, rather than impose, values. This is because internalizing is a process, while imposing is simply an act. But nothing else will do. Imposing values is a Band-Aid over a wound that will grow wider every year. Either values are a part of the child, or they are nothing.

There's no doubt that you can produce a godly veneer if you choose to impose values, and you may even be able to make this imposition last past high school and college—perhaps even to the end of *your* life. But it probably won't last to the end of your child's life. Like Pavlovian dogs, your children can be behavior-modified and assertively disciplined until their instant and mindless responses impress your friends and family and woo converts to the idea of parental despotism. But will their values disappear when you do?

Our daughter Laura hated getting up for school when she was in first grade. We could have simply imposed the requirement to get up on time onto this little child. Instead, we chose to teach her what Scripture says about the ever-present biblical personage, the sluggard. We didn't do it just one time but went through a process that took months. We got her an alarm clock of her own, so that she would have the necessary tools to do it *herself*.

The result? Laura now gets up before any of us and is reading before most people shut off their alarms. She doesn't even have to *set* her alarm anymore. It's become a habit. She doesn't do it because we commanded her or because she's afraid of what we'll do or say, but simply because she has chosen to rise early. It's an act of her own will.

Our son Peter was a first-class storyteller, with all the hyperbole and embellishments that a spinner of yarns could want. But it was difficult for him when he was younger to pick out the difference between telling stories and telling lies. We could have threatened his life and limb if he ever said anything untrue. But we chose the process route instead.

We taught him what Scripture says about being a man of integrity. We discussed and observed together the consequences of lying and the benefits of telling the truth. This process has taken years, but I believe that Peter is now a young man willing to tell the truth even at great personal cost.

Evaluating Their Progress

One of the best measures of how you're doing in this area is to watch what your children are interested in and what they aren't. Take the issue of friends. If you're like most parents, you want your children to have excellent friends. You can see pretty clearly which of their peers are godly and which ones are godless. If, no matter what you say, your children keep leaning toward and pushing to have godless friends, and you feel like you're in a war of wills, you're imposing—and losing. If, instead, your children with their own judgment consistently pick godly friends and avoid the godless, you're internalizing—and winning.

There are certainly times when commands are called for—when the child has, for example, disobeyed a clearcut rule or is heading for danger. But whenever possible, choose the route of internalization over the easier route of imposition. Teach a child to respond only to a command, and you've taught him godliness for a moment;

teach a child to respond also to the truth, and you've taught him godliness for a lifetime.
Be wise. Internalize.

Establishing Holiness _____ *in Your Home* _____

Television

It has been said that television as a medium is doomed forever to mediocrity—and that would be fine if it just wasn't a sewer, too. Sometimes, trying to find a decent television program or movie is akin to trying to find a chicken sandwich in a garbage can.

That said, the real challenge is to distinguish between the amazing technology that television really is and the obscene and preposterous ways in which it is so often being used. I'm glad that I have modern knives to use in our kitchen, even as I'm appalled by a person using a knife to kill someone.

It is totally astounding that we can sit in the comfort of our homes and watch political debates, educational programs, fine old (and a few new) movies, a charging elephant herd in Africa, and a Grinch stealing Christmas.

Certainly, people, including children, sitting in front of a television for hours can be a problem—even if they're only watching good things. But I think that as long as the supply of quality material was there, even Thomas Jefferson would have a hard time dragging himself away from the wonder of it all.

But just because you have a television doesn't mean you have to watch every prime-time show or movie—or *anything at all*! Set some clear guidelines, starting with the cable channels you won't get and the programs you'll never watch. Have a "commercial-avoidance" strategy. Commit to each other that if you've made it through all but the last five minutes of a two-hour movie and it turns morally "ugly," you'll turn it off without batting an eye.

If you just can't control it, then by all means get rid of the thing. Jesus told us to gouge out our eye or cut off our hand and throw them away if they offend us (see Matthew 5:29-30), so pitching a television should be an obvious choice if our hearts are at stake.

Appeasement

Winston Churchill described appeasement as a process of feeding an alligator with the hope that he'll eat you last. Many parents are raising little alligators, and the easiest thing in the world is to appease them.

The process of appeasement can begin when any problem or evil creeps into your child's life. When you see something in his life that you know to be unscriptural and which offends your sense of right and wrong in however subtle a way, you have a choice to make.

The right choice is to deal with it in a straightforward and loving way, helping the child through the problem quickly and deliberately, using all of the tools of God and the authority He has delegated to you. You can begin to internalize values on this point, hiding the Word in his heart so he won't sin against God (see Psalm 119:11). In the meantime, you can safeguard his life with clear commands.

This is the way that wins. Don't let any junk get off the ground, and you can fight it before it becomes a part of his life.

The other choice is really destructive. For whatever reason—sentimentality, cowardice, ignorance of the ruinous nature of evil, whatever—you decide to allow the attitude or action to continue, but you decide to "control" it through various restrictions.

The argument goes something like this: I can only do so much to control a child. If I'm too tough on this, it might produce even more rebellion. Tough standards will only make the thing more attractive anyway. This world has become too evil to block it all out. He's going to have to learn how to deal with this for himself, in any case, and surely some restrictions are better than the nothing that other parents are doing.

This, folks, is rationalization, and an acceptance of the worst that worldly wisdom has to offer. It only places boundaries around your child's evil behavior when you know that the behavior itself is wrong. There's no way this path can be blessed. It's not as good as internalizing. It's not even as good as imposing.

Eli the priest received one of the strongest punishments anywhere in Scripture because he knew about his sons' sins yet "failed to restrain them" (see 1 Samuel 3:11-14). God said He "would judge his family forever." What a warning for us (see 1 Corinthians 10:6)!

The result of appeasement will likely be at least as bad as if you had set *no* restrictions on the attitude or action. First and worst, you'll have left your child on an evil road that leads to all kinds of death and misery. He'll probably still view you as a tyrant for putting any restrictions on him, because this kind of "freedom" produces a thirst for more of the same. You'll have taught him that a little evil is okay and that it's all right to live outside of God's boundaries. His disrespect for your lukewarmness, and finally for you, will grow and perhaps even devour your relationship.

And the "joke" is on you, because it won't stop what he's doing and it won't pacify him. God never called parents to control evil in their children; He expects us to work with Him to totally weed it out. Scripture says that parents who love their son are *"careful* to discipline him" (Proverbs 13:24). This means that you think about it, and then do it.

It's the only way to live, and the only way that works. No surrender. No compromise. And no appeasement.

Taking the Fifth Amendment

What goes through your mind when you hear something true but awful about someone you've always respected?

Whether it's George Washington or your Aunt Susie, your reaction probably runs toward disappointment—perhaps even bitter disappointment, if your respect was particularly high and the story was particularly low. At some point, especially if the story involves an offense against you or someone else you love, your disappointment can turn to anger or even hatred. That's why Scripture says: "He who covers over an offense promotes love, but whoever repeats the matter separates close friends" (Proverbs 17:9).

Filth dredged from a person's past can really damage his friendship with many people, even close friends. Unfortunately, there's too much repeating and too little covering over in God's family. After a person has requested forgiveness from the offended person and God, his time in the spotlight of guilt should end. We must stop ruining others, and their friendships and loves, by passing things along in public displays or private conversations. You wouldn't want others to do it to you; who in heaven gave you the right to do it to someone else?

This matter becomes crucial with regard to your children. You're the pride of your children, one of their highest models on earth and their continual example. If someone—be it pastor or elder or prominent Christian or friend or acquaintance or enemy—starts spreading around some of your past sin, what do you think it will do to your children?

It could ruin their opinion of you. It might even ruin them. Muck sucks people to a lower level. Always.

Be careful of what your children hear. Who knows how much damage has been done by grandparents or other relatives telling children what rotten little beasts their parents were when they were younger? Or what scars are left when a friend or enemy demolishes a parent with reckless words in the presence of his children? God knows. So do the children.

Parents can also get into plenty of trouble by sharing in a serious way the details of their past sins with others in the presence of their children or with their children directly. Hearing about what you were like when you were a dead person just isn't going to elevate their view of the possibilities of the Christian life. Your motive—sharing these truths to help others see that you're only human, or to warn them what to avoid—might be understandable, but it's wrong.

Some people reading this will disagree. "Nobody should pretend to be perfect," they'll say. I agree. The Bible says, "If we claim to be without sin, we deceive ourselves and the truth is not in us" (1 John 1:8). Admit to any and all that you're not perfect. But *don't* admit to the details of the past. Weren't you dead in your sins, a spiritual corpse in a spiritual casket? Why not talk about something valuable—like *life*?

Do me a favor. Do those around you a favor. Do yourself a favor. Do your children a favor.

Take the fifth amendment.

___ *To Everything, a Season* ___

One of the most critical areas of holiness is that of moral purity. You *must* teach your children to learn to relate to their bodies in a godly, spiritual, and balanced way (see 1 Thessalonians 4:3-7).

Parents of an earlier day may have erred on the side of giving too little teaching concerning the importance of the body and a proper view of sexuality. You don't want to be in this category. Talk to your children about these things a little at a time, as they're ready. Dads need to

take the lead in this. When children are little, tell them
enough to protect them from the twisted people who
drive through neighborhoods. When children are older,
give them the high biblical vision of marriage, not just
the biological facts.

Self-Discovery

This may come as a surprise to you, but your children
will eventually discover that they have bodies. If they're
really astute, they'll also discover that some things bring
them pleasure and other things bring them pain. Avoidance of pain comes naturally to children.
Avoidance of pleasure doesn't.
From their earliest moments, children find that certain things are pleasurable and so build them into their
habits of life. At first, everything is taste-tested. Later,
everything not hung from the ceiling will get looked at,
listened to, smelled, touched, and very probably dis-
mantled. It's all new to them, and they're just fascinated.
Inevitably they'll discover their bodies, in the tub or the
bed or the backyard. What they do with this discovery
and, more importantly, what *you* do with their discovery
can have an effect on them so dramatic that you cannot
afford to avoid the issue.
Many parents in the past, and perhaps many parents
even today, simply pretended as though this discovery
just wasn't going to happen. "Nice" people didn't discuss such things, and *certainly* not with children. They
left their children to discover the truth about their bodies
on their own behind the barn or in the backseat of a car or
on their wedding night. Today, however, some parents
may be telling their children too much, too soon, too
unrelated to the role their bodies will play in living a
successful, powerful, and joyous life.
These parents may admit their awareness of their
child's self-discovery and allow it to go on without comment. In this day of no acknowledged sin or folly or

restraint, some may even encourage it passively, by allowing unrestricted television or movies or friendships; or actively, by things too despicable to mention. There might be a feeling that "it's only natural," and, of course, they're right. But that's been the problem ever since man cut the natural away from the supernatural.

One other possible response is open irritation or even anger, righteous or otherwise. This can send a thousand destructive and confusing signals to a child but will probably not discourage the child's action, and may, in fact, lead to more sin and guilt. It attempts to force a value on the child from the outside when it's beyond your ability to enforce it. You must internalize a godly concept of sexuality.

Sexuality Is Created Good

So what do you do with your child's self-discovery program? Do you ignore it? No. Encourage it? No. Become angry and forbid it? No. Tell him it's good? No. Tell him it's bad? No.

"Well," you say, "that clinches it. I suspected all along that the only way to deal with this explosive issue was to lock my children in their bedrooms until they're 80."

But you can't ignore this self-discovery. And, while innocent discovery of self may not be a sin, unrestrained discovery will almost certainly lead to that conclusion. The truth is, their sexuality was created to be a good thing, but it can be used in many bad ways.

And this is exactly what your children should be taught: Their sexuality is a good thing. Used rightly, sexuality is a blessing; used wrongly, it's a terrible sin that will devour their spirits *and* their bodies. You can show examples from Scripture to your children: from the exquisite poetry of the Song of Solomon and the love of Ruth and Boaz, to the hideous story of the men of Sodom (see Genesis 18–19) and the empty life of the woman of Samaria (see John 4:1-26).

Early in your children's lives, if you see them engaging in self-stimulation or perhaps even innocent activities with others, you should show them that God created their bodies and made them in such a way that they can experience many pleasures. But just because they *can* doesn't mean that they *should*.

Tell them how wonderful sexual pleasure can and will be—at the right time, in the right place, with the right marriage partner. They must believe that if used in God's way, their bodies and their desires will be able to be satisfied. Teach the truth to the girls that "like a gold ring in a pig's snout is a beautiful woman who shows no discretion" (Proverbs 11:22). Instruct the boys that improper sexual activity gives their "best strength to others" (Proverbs 5:7-14).

And I want to give you, especially dads, a strong word of encouragement. Smother your children with affection—good affection, godly affection. So many young girls in trouble with boys and so many young men struggling with homosexuality never had this. Smother them early and often. Use softness or kidding to "enforce" bedtime kisses and hugs. When they're older it might seem awkward, but do it anyway. No gift that you can buy with money is as valuable as this one.

___ *Indignation* ___

James Russell Lowell said, "The capacity of indignation makes an essential part of the outfit of every honest man."

If your children are going to walk a holy walk in an unholy world, they're going to need to know when and how to be indignant.

It's possibly true that *you* don't know when and how to be indignant, so the first thing to do is define it.

Indignation is "anger excited by that which is unworthy, base, or disgraceful; righteous wrath."

Righteous wrath. If I can have that, I have one more thing that makes me an imitator of God, for God displays mighty indignation many times in Scripture. For most of us, wrath comes pretty easily; it's the righteousness part that causes the rub.

What are the key ingredients of this crowning attribute? They can be seen in the actions of Jesus the two times He cleared the temple of the money changers (see John 2:13-17; Mark 11:15-17).

Jesus was offended because God the Father was offended. Your children shouldn't become indignant about someone taking their toys. A right purpose is related to a direct and unrelenting assault against *God*, not against your children, by someone who doesn't fear God.

Jesus didn't participate in the sales show. Your children must not be participating in the offensive act if they want their integrity to shine and their indignation to be righteous.

Jesus displayed His indignation at the right time: "on reaching Jerusalem." Your children should become indignant only when other efforts have failed; then they should move without hesitation.

Jesus prepared for His effort. Contrary to the picture of indignation being wild anger, Jesus took the time to make a whip. Your children should prepare themselves with the whip of Scripture, to have it ready so they can drive out the enemies of God.

Jesus didn't politely ask those in the area to leave. He "began driving out those who were buying and selling there." If your children are sure of their position, they too will know that debates and requests will not work on those who are spitting in God's face.

Jesus carried out His effort with lots of action and few words, and He wasn't gentle with either. His words were warnings and quotations of Scripture. Your children should know and present the scriptural reason for their action, and act without further ado.

Jesus' zeal was so overwhelming that His disciples remembered the prophecy: "Zeal for your house consumes me" (Psalm 69:9). How many children—or adults, for that matter—have you known who had *that* kind of zeal? *Jesus offered no apologies.* Neither should you. Neither should your children. It's the world that owes *God* the apology.

What should make you indignant? How about millions of slaughtered unborn babies? Stores selling pornography not too far from your house? Newspapers printing the horrible details of countless murders while editorializing on more leniency for the murderer? Local schools being willing to teach *anything* as long as it's not what *you* believe?

Write some letters. Make some phone calls. Spend some time and money fighting for right. Make a sign and put your faith on the line. And involve your children in all of this. Let them see righteous indignation in action.

If you don't think there's anything unworthy, base, or disgraceful going on, then you can forget this section until something comes along.

Or until you wake up.

You can be holy as God is holy. Your children can be holy as God is holy.

Do this, and watch the world change around your family.

8

Stability

Fiction: All change is a normal part of life, and you might as well get used to it.

Fact: Jesus Christ is the same yesterday, and today, and forever (Hebrews 13:8).

There have been few nations in which the people were less rooted and less stable than in the United States, a land full of restless nomads.

Nomads? Why, we aren't a nation of tent dwellers and camel riders! But *nomads* are those who "have no fixed location, but wander from place to place."

We wander from house to house, community to community, state to state, job to job, church to church, marriage to marriage. We wander as much as another group that spent 40 years wandering around a desert, creating our own desert where nothing living can take root.

There's just not much continuity. In business, for example, the willingness of managers and others to uproot and move from job to job within a company or from company to company is actually viewed as an asset rather than a liability. And yet, if you ask these people who they think would be most effective, a brilliant manager at a company for only a year or a good manager for 25 years, most would probably say the latter.

That's because there's no substitute for stability, consistency, and continuity. Not brilliance or motivation or

money or possessions, not activities or programs or
birthday parties. Nothing. If you don't give your family
strong and stable roots, you haven't given them anything that will last.

__ Stable Parents __

It has been said that parenting is the only skilled job
in the world that requires no prior experience.

A parent is dealing with an entirely new situation,
requiring a vast array of skills for many years. And
although there are many vital principles that remain the
same, each child will require yet another skillful and
varied application. Add to this the fact that you're
changing at the same time, and being a stable parent can
seem impossible!

But your children desperately need you to be stable
and consistent in your dealings with them. They need to
be able to *count* on things, year after year, regardless of
circumstances.

Sadly, you *can* erroneously choose to be no more than
a physical parent, simply providing food and shelter,
and letting "nature take its course." The state of parenting in the United States has deteriorated in many ways to
this maintenance level. Your children will probably still
grow up, and they will probably not hate you. You must
understand, however, that your substitution of the
material for the spiritual will not be appreciated by your
child. He'll resent your omission even as he holds his
hand out for more.

To help your children with their need for stability,
you have to start *within* yourself. Are you an up-and-
down Christian? You don't have the right to be this kind
of Christian, either with God or your children. Run to
your God like a rock badger runs into the rocks (see
Proverbs 30:26), and let God stabilize your life. You can
be like your heavenly Father, "who does not change like
shifting shadows" (James 1:17).

__ *Zapped!* __

If you agree that you must be a stable parent, working consistently in all areas of life to develop stable Christian children, where does your work begin?

With your marriage.

Even if you follow the rest of the advice in this book, you can still zap your children's ability to be what God wants them to be by missing the lesson of Ephesians 5:21-33. Your attempts to train your children will be less than fully effective if you, as a wife, don't submit to and respect your husband. You must do these things—all day, every day, even though it's hard, even though your husband might abuse his authority or not always be "worthy" of your respect.

In the same way, your attempts to train your children can be largely a waste of time if you, as a husband, don't love your wife as your own body, giving yourself up for *her* benefit, making her holy, clean, radiant, and blameless. You *must* do this, even if she isn't "beautiful," even if she doesn't submit to you or respect you.

There is balance here, of course—a need for mutuality and integrity. For example, a wife is *not* to submit in areas where her husband is leading her or the family away from the Lord (see Acts 4:19), but only "as is fitting in the Lord" (Colossians 3:18). But the more complete the picture, the better it will be for the children.

God frequently gives us earthly symbols of heavenly truths. In watching your marriage relationship, your children will come to understand the profound mystery of Christ and the church. If you want your children to see how they should relate to Christ, let them see you moms relating in a submissive, respectful way to their fathers. If you want your children to see how Christ would relate to them, let them see you dads relating in a loving, sacrificial way to their mothers.

Can you see how absolutely indispensable this is? If either parent doesn't do his or her part, the children get only half the picture. Either they can be less willing to submit to Christ, or they won't be fully ready to accept the love that Christ has for them.

It's been said that the greatest thing a dad can do for his children is to love their mother. It sounds good, but it isn't true. The greatest thing a dad can do for his children is to love God.

But loving their mother is a mighty good number two.

___ Two Masters ___

Being a stable, consistent parent who is in right relationship with your spouse is very good. But it's not enough. You've got another problem.

There are two of you.

Why is this a problem? Jesus gives us the principle: "No one can serve two masters. Either he will hate the one and love the other, or he will be devoted to the one and despise the other" (Matthew 6:24). "No one" includes your children.

You're two people; you look for all the world like two masters, you can sound like two masters, you can *be* two masters. But you've got to speak as one *person*, one *master*, or you're dead as parents. How on earth can two people pull this off?

Because of something else that Jesus said: "For this reason a man will leave his father and mother and be united to his wife, and the two will become one flesh. *So they are no longer two, but one*" (Mark 10:7-8).

You can avoid the two-master problem, because in God's eyes you *are* one master, you *are* one person. If you'll learn to put this great truth into practice— consistently speaking with one voice—you'll keep your children out of a terrible dilemma. And if you don't do these things, you'll be a house divided against itself.

And your home will surely fall (see Luke 11:17).

___ *Staying Home* ___

And now, the $64,000 question: How can you have a stable home, if nobody's there?

In many cases, parents assaulted by the ravages of taxes, inflation, and poor education have had to give up much of their parenting time to others. In other cases, some have voluntarily delegated the one job on which they'll be judged by everyone who knows them.

Working mothers have rapidly become the norm. From "having to work" just to pay bills, to "having to work" to get a bigger piece of the American Dream, to saying, "I wasn't cut out to stay home and take care of kids," a large percentage of women have lowered their vision of motherhood.

Dads won't get any relief here either. Where have you been while your child was being raised outside of your home? Do you think Scripture says that your sole responsibility is your job, and your wife's job is everything else? If the two of you fail in this effort, whose head do you think goes into the godly guillotine first?

Many years ago, in an essay entitled "Father," my daughter Laura had this to say: "He finds plenty of time to spend with us, too. . . . He usually stays home in the evenings. My dad is wise." I didn't know that staying home was wise, until I read that essay. I do now.

One or the other of you needs to be home when your children are. Scripture encourages mothers "to be busy at home" (Titus 2:5). This doesn't mean that a mom can't run a business—even a substantial business—out of her home (look at the Proverbs 31 woman). But her home is her base. And we dads need to leave the materialism quest to those who belong to the world. Many of us need to reduce our time on career and outside activities, so that we can increase our time with our wives and children.

And what about the single parent? How I feel for you! I know that many of you are not parenting alone by choice, and that this section could be difficult, even heart-wrenching, to read. You must work to support your family, and other sources of income (child support, life insurance proceeds, savings, etc.) may be limited or nonexistent.

But the *spirit* of this section is still for you. Try to work from home, if you can and as much as you can. Try to have your children as close to work as possible, so you can lunch with them and even look in on them. Try to work less hours if you can somehow make it on less pay. See if a loved one will shop for you so you can spend that time with your children instead. Plan your life with the certainty that more of you is far better for your children than anything else—except God and His Word.

Dads and moms, there really is no place like home. Be there.

___ *The Horror of Divorce* ___

"'I hate divorce,' says the LORD God of Israel" (Malachi 2:16). Me, too.

This is an age when many men and women, including church leaders, have come to the conclusion that divorce is acceptable, often necessary, and at times even the best option. And of course, if divorce is okay, then remarriage must be okay, too.

But a recent secular book, *The Case Against Divorce*, shows that the world is beginning to see the horror of divorce, perhaps even more clearly than some Christians who should know better.

God's View on Divorce and Remarriage

God says no divorce (see Malachi 2:13-16; Mark 10:9; Romans 7:2).

Remarriage isn't even a legitimate word, biblically speaking. Since God never accepts men putting asunder what He has joined together, then two who have become one *are* one in His eyes. Marriage to someone else isn't called *remarriage* in the Bible; it's called *adultery* (see Mark 10:11-12; Luke 16:18; Romans 7:3).

Reconciliation with your original marriage partner isn't remarriage, either; it's just agreeing to continue a marriage that you were bound to by God and your vow all along. Sexual sin outside of marriage does not make way for breaking the covenant, but for forgiveness and restoration. An outstanding example of this kind of reconciliation is that of the prophet Hosea with his faithless wife, Gomer (see Hosea 1–3).

And what about the "exceptions"?

The only time we see the so-called unfaithfulness exception is in Matthew 5:31-32 and 19:3-9, in a book which was written originally to Jews who knew the Law. *Unfaithfulness*, as defined by God's Law, means forbidden marriages (see Leviticus 18) or betrothal (engagement) unfaithfulness (see Deuteronomy 22). Jesus was saying that a lawful marriage cannot be broken—and that an *unlawful* marriage is not a marriage at all.

And what about the unbeliever leaving (see 1 Corinthians 7:15-16)? Paul was writing to people who had become believers after they were already married, but whose spouses were still unbelievers. He tells them to stick with it. If the unbeliever leaves, the believer is "not bound." In other words, the believer is no longer forced to live in a day-to-day unequal yoking. But divorce and remarriage are never mentioned in the chapter. In fact, Paul closes the chapter by reiterating that married people are bound for life (verse 39). And this chapter isn't for a believer who deliberately marries an unbeliever; that act is a sin in its own right (see 1 Corinthians 7:39; 2 Corinthians 6:14-17). Ezra 9–10 is also sober reading on this subject.

Don't ever consider a divorce. Emotional and physical separation from abuse, yes, but divorce, never. It
will certainly devastate your life. If you throw a God-
instituted relationship back into His face and go your
own way, how can you expect anything else?

Effects on Your Children

But perhaps even worse than the devastation in your
own life will be that wreaked upon your children, your
grandchildren, and your great-grandchildren. Your children will be raised in a strange, unbiblical way, as they
live only with one parent or become a living beach ball
tossed back and forth between two parents. They will
also have a hard time accepting that your love is unfailing and permanent. After all, didn't you make a pledge
to their other parent that you would never stop loving
him or her?

The decision to divorce has another potential effect
that will pound through your descendants' lives for
decades, even centuries. You will have taught them by
your example that God's Word is a lie, that actions don't
have consequences, that vows are nothing (see Ecclesiastes 5:4-6), that relationships exist only for our personal
gratification, and that marriage is a triviality. No matter
what you *say*, how do you think *they're* going to look at
marriage and divorce in their own lives?

Marrying someone else just compounds the sin and
confusion. Who is my daddy? Who is my mommy? To
whom do I submit? It's just not God's way.

If you're divorced, ask God's and your partner's and
your children's forgiveness. Do everything you can to be
reconciled to the other half of you. If your spouse has
married another or simply won't be reconciled, then you
must not remarry. Spend much time teaching your children the truth about divorce, how wrong it was, and
why you're still going to be faithful to your covenant by

not marrying another. Show your children your sorrow as you show them the consequences of this divorce in your own and other people's lives.

For our God's sake, believe Him on this one.

___ On the Road Again ___

Our culture has always had a measure of mobility, but since the end of World War II we have become a rootless society. How can there be any sense of community, belonging, or accountability in a nation where nobody stops moving long enough to meet his neighbors?

People will move almost at the drop of a hat. They'll move for a better job, fancier title, more money, a bigger house, a better climate, more convenient access to leisure activities. Often our transience is the result of "greed, which is *idolatry*" (Colossians 3:5). Paul tells us that "the love of money is a root of all kinds of evil. Some people, eager for money, have wandered from the faith" (1 Timothy 6:10). Sad to say, it causes some to just wander.

More often than not, though, Christians simply lack an understanding of the biblical picture of living deeply within the family of God. Relationships with brothers and sisters in Christ, rooted in God Himself and knit together over time, are the foundation of stability. God Himself is interested in birthing and maturing deep relationships between people that can speak to and affect those around them, and can continue to speak for generations and into eternity itself.

The process of learning to relate closely to another person over time can bring friction, tension, and challenge, but these can be the very things that build our Christian maturity. The end result of "sticking it out" with another's frailties is yet a richer understanding of the kind of unfailing love that God has for us and wants us to have with each other.

When you have worked at a relationship long enough, you can end up with a rich tapestry of hearts woven together. This can bring joy in the midst of the hardships of living in a fallen world and sunshine into the gloom. With God, and a relationship (or two, if you are really blessed) like this, you don't need much of anything else, except maybe a little food.

Although there is such a thing as a move prompted by God, if you're honest, you have to admit that many moves don't have much to do with a vision from the Lord. That ripping up of roots will not benefit people who need roots to grow in stable soil.

Transience will teach your children:

- It doesn't pay to get close to anybody, because either you or the other person won't be here in a year or two anyway.
- Moving around for more money is a high priority. (Don't be surprised when they move away from you.)
- People can do what they want, because nobody knows them here.
- We don't need to fix broken relationships; there are plenty of other acquaintances to spend time with.
- Extended family doesn't have much value. Grand-parents send birthday cards and Christmas presents and call long distance.

A lot of bad lessons. A terrible heritage. But you can stop it. Even Paul, a missionary, walked away from an open door of opportunity because his friend Titus wasn't there to share the work and joy with him (see 2 Corinthians 2:12-13).

Because we and a few other families have chosen to settle in the same place, I have gotten close to a number of people with whom I share a deep personal connection and mutual investment. One is my true daughter in the faith, Maryl Jan. We have come to a point where we can quickly understand each other's problems, encourage and comfort one another, help each other with "blind spots," and share rich spiritual insights and joyous closeness in the Lord. A relationship like this is worth much more than any amount of gold and silver. And this kind of connection can only come with time.

God Himself is interested in birthing and maturing deep relationships between people that can speak to and affect those around them, and can continue to speak for generations and into eternity itself.

You can be the family who puts down roots and says, "This is it." You can become a solid part of your community—maybe, for a while, the only solid part. You can teach and show your children how to develop and keep deep relationships for a lifetime. You can commit to your church and involve yourself with people you can grow old with.

___ *Responsibility* ___

A great number of parents are now giving their children the "freedom" of being an adult without giving them minimum responsibilities. Children are allowed to experience things that are beyond their comprehension and exceed their wisdom, while nothing is demanded of them in return—or at all.

Does God support letting children reap where they haven't sown? Does Scripture support the materialistic creed of giving your child a "better" life than you had? Or that childhood should be free from any restraints that would spoil the fun? No, you say; and I agree. Then what is it that's allowing us to produce a generation of anarchists?

It involves parental apathy, ignorance, lack of love, and disregard for the office of parent itself. These things add up to abdication of parental responsibility and, as a natural consequence, the abdication of responsibility and responsible behavior on the part of the child as well. Can you imagine this irresponsible new generation as *parents*?

You must exercise responsibility in the things that God has given you. The example you set for your children in this area is more important than the responsibilities you assign them. If you get up and go to work when you don't feel like it, cook dinner when you have a splitting headache, take in a hurting family member when you don't have room, you'll be teaching responsibility, loud and clear.

And don't miss giving your children responsibility. It isn't cruel and heartless to give them things to do; it's *vital*. If you can escape from the world's view that children should be allowed to "live it up" all the time, you might actually be able to see the truth that mindless entertainment never built anyone's character. Booker T. Washington reminded us of this: "Few things help an individual more than to place responsibility upon him, and to let him know that you trust him."

My son Peter once said to me, "Dad, I'm the only kid in the neighborhood who has to do chores." I gave him the only appropriate answer that a loving parent can give: "You're welcome."

__ *The Harvest of Discipline* __

I didn't make discipline a separate chapter because discipline is the whole process of making a disciple. I chose to include it here, because consistent discipline is such an important part of a stable life.

The *attitude* of discipline is the key. One of the main reasons we have so many mediocre Christians is that they were raised by somebody's gimmicks rather than by a parent's godly approach to discipline. And what is the godly approach?

As conveyed to your child, it should sound something like this:

> I'm your father, and I love you more deeply than you may ever know. There's nothing you can ever say or do to make me stop loving you. I want to spend my time thinking about you in two ways: First, to present you with challenges so that you will be a powerful Christian; second, to immerse myself in thinking creatively about how I can shower you with blessings. If you respond to these things, you will find the way of life in God a shorter, softer path (Proverbs 6:23; 10:17).
>
> But since I love you, if you reject these things you'll force me to spend my time thinking about you in two other directions. First, my challenges will turn into punishments designed to shake you off the wrong path. Second, I'll have to think creatively about how I can withdraw my blessings. Actions have consequences, and I love you too much to let you be a fool. I'll still try to help you grow in Christ but you'll be doing it on the longer, harder path.

Our children were resisting taking care of a responsibility that we felt was important. Pam and I had tried all of the "tricks"—do this, ground that, withdraw this, nag there—all to no avail. Then I realized that I was giving them the output of my own shaky thinking, without even knowing clearly what I wanted them to learn or why. I was fighting a battle of details when I needed to let them see the heart that was prompting the details. When we conveyed why we required them to do the thing they had been resisting, and that it was excellent training for their lives, their comprehension of our love and discipline was much more complete.

God shows us His attitude in Hebrews 12:5-11:

> And you have forgotten that word of encour-
> agement that addresses you as sons: "My son, do
> not make light of the Lord's discipline, and do not
> lose heart when he rebukes you, because the Lord
> disciplines those he loves, and he punishes every-
> one he accepts as a son." Endure hardship as disci-
> pline; God is treating you as sons. . . . God disciplines
> us for our good, that we may share in his holiness.
> No discipline seems pleasant at the time, but pain-
> ful. Later on, however, it produces a harvest of
> righteousness and peace for those who have been
> trained by it.

Convey your approach to discipline clearly to your
children. Help them see that discipline will produce a
gigantic and marvelous harvest of righteousness and
peace in their lives. They're being built into something
strong: "Therefore, strengthen your feeble arms and
weak knees. 'Make level paths for your feet,' so that the
lame may not be disabled, but rather healed" (Hebrews
12:12-13).

It'll be a lot easier for them to head in that direction
when they see the goal and not just the details.

Is there a place for physical discipline? Definitely.
But it should be part of a total package that seeks inward
change and not just outward conformance (see Proverbs
17:10).

Discipline your children in the full sense of the word.
And remember that you want to win the battle on discipline before your children know there is a war.

In the midst of a rootless and nomadic culture, you
can give your children the gift of stability—in your marriage, in your family, in your church.

Believe me, it's a gift the generations that follow will
still be opening in a hundred years.

9

Confidence

Fiction: We can't expect all of our prayers to be answered—sometimes the answer is yes, sometimes it's maybe, sometimes it's no.

Fact: You may ask me for anything in my name, and I will do it (John 14:14).

In a world that's falling apart, there are at least three or four thousand things that could drive you, as a parent, into an absolute panic. From a child falling and hitting his head to being kidnapped off the street where he lives, the possible disasters awaiting your family can dominate your attention. And if you're not careful, they will.

Not only can this fear cause you to sin against the Lord and ruin much of your relationship with your children, but it can also be a devastatingly effective method of teaching your children the fear of man, bad news, and sudden disaster. You can talk about your confidence in the Lord until your voice gives out, but if you live fear, you'll teach fear. And fear is disobedience to Jesus (see Matthew 6:25,31,34; 10:19).

The basic question is pretty simple: Who is really and ultimately responsible for the safety of your children? Given the grotesque culture in which we live, if the answer is "I am," your children are in big trouble. The only way that this could possibly work is if you are omnipresent and omnipotent, and I suspect that you aren't.

159

But God really *does* promise peace and safety for your children; you *can* rest from your worry and fear. It is possible for you to obey His command not to worry. You are able to place your children in God's hands and have the certainty that they won't be dropped.

What are God's promises on this important issue?

> • He who fears the LORD has a secure fortress, and for his children it will be a refuge (Proverbs 14:26).

God didn't put your child into a storm sewer; He put him or her into your family. Your family's safety, spiritual *and* physical, begins with eliminating all fear except the fear of the Lord (see Acts 9:31; 10:34-35; 2 Corinthians 5:11; 7:15; Philippians 2:12; 1 Peter 1:17). Roosevelt said, "The only thing we have to fear is fear itself." Nonsense. The only thing we have to fear is God.

> • The Lord says in Proverbs that whoever listens to wisdom "will live in safety and be at ease, without fear of harm" (Proverbs 1:33).

By listening and learning "you will go on your way in safety, and your foot will not stumble; when you lie down, you will not be afraid; when you lie down, your sleep will be sweet. Have *no* fear of sudden disaster or of the ruin that overtakes the wicked, for the LORD will be your confidence and will keep your foot from being snared" (Proverbs 3:23-26). You must learn wisdom for your own safety. You must teach your children wisdom for *their* safety. "Follow my decrees and be careful to obey my laws, and you will live safely in the land" (Leviticus 25:18). And if we ignore God's Law, God says He will *ignore our children* (see Hosea 4:6)!

> • A prudent man sees danger and takes refuge (Proverbs 22:3).

But where? "The name of the LORD is a strong tower; the righteous run to it and *are safe*" (Proverbs 18:10). We as believers have taken the name of our Father. We are His heirs, to whom He says: "If anyone does attack you, it will not be my doing; whoever attacks you *will surrender to you*" (Isaiah 54:15).

- To the *faithful* you show yourself faithful (Psalm 18:25).

"The LORD preserves the *faithful*" (Psalm 31:23). He "will not forsake his *faithful* ones" (Psalm 37:28). "He guards the lives of his *faithful* ones" (Psalm 97:10). "No harm befalls the *righteous*" (Proverbs 12:21). Do you get the picture? Calling yourself a believer is not enough. If you want God's protection in this life, you have to live by faith, in obeying His commands and in claiming His promises.

It should be pointed out that godly prudence must be exercised in the supervision of your children. The balance is in trusting your children to God first and then having your children in the right place at the right time. Trusting God isn't an excuse to let your prudence go to lunch early. It's wrong to think that your children are totally in your hands; but it's also wrong to think that they're not in your hands at all.

Perhaps the most important thing that will be accomplished by this joyous way of life is that you won't teach your children to fear what those in the world fear (see 1 Peter 3:14). Think of it: If your children fear nothing but God, they will share a primary attribute with someone very, very special—they'll be like Christ.

_ *Apply Faith to Fear* _

People who know about God can be really amazing on the subject of worry and fear. We fear men and do the things we shouldn't do before God, when we should fear God and do the things we should do before men. We fear things over which we have no control, like nuclear war, cancer, and muggers, while we don't fear things over which we have control, like the consequences of disobedience to God.

Any fear other than the fear of God is misplaced and can bring upon us the very thing we dread. Job said, "What I feared has come upon me; what I dreaded has happened to me. I have no peace, no quietness; I have no rest, but only turmoil" (Job 3:25-26).

Why is this? Because fear and worry are disobedience to God.

Fear indicates a lack of faith in God. In fact, fear *is* a lack of faith in God. We can spout fountains of words about how God is all-knowing, all-powerful, and all-loving. But the real question is, do we really believe that God is sovereign—in total control—and that nothing can touch us except by His permission? Isaiah 8:12-14 says: "Do not call conspiracy everything that these people call conspiracy; do not fear what they fear, and do not dread it. The LORD Almighty is the one you are to regard as holy, he is the one you are to fear, he is the one you are to dread, *and he will be a sanctuary.*"

We have to get this point over to our children. When they come to us with their fears, we need to encourage them to run into the arms of God, to cling tightly to Him, and to say with the psalmist, "When I am afraid, I will trust in you" (Psalm 56:3). We need to warn them that if they give these fears a home they're disobeying God. And we need to tell them, clearly and lovingly, that their fears are ungodly.

When Laura was 11, the enemy assaulted her with many fears and doubts about her faith. I think he does this with any child he sees as a possible threat to his disintegrating kingdom. With Laura, most of the attacks came in the middle of the night.

I still thank God for how He worked during that time. With God's real help, Laura and I developed a trust and communication between us. When she would awake, trembling, she would make her way down to our bedroom and knock on the door. Miraculously, God woke me ahead of her knock *every time*. I was already alert and ready for her when she came to the door.

She would come in and sit by the side of my bed in the dark. She would whisper in my ear about the turmoil the enemy was pouring into her. And God would bring Scriptures to my mind for her, and I would comfort her and pray for her. She got victory in this war, and we got closer as a result.

You can do it, too. Ask God to alert you when your children are being bombarded, and to help you be ready. He didn't fail me. He won't fail you.

When our children come to us with their fears, we need to encourage them to run into the arms of God, to cling tightly to Him, and to say with the psalmist, "When I am afraid, I will trust in you."

The "experts" have a different solution, which can sound pretty good. They tell us to discuss the child's fears with him, help him rationalize his fears, and teach him to work through them in his own mind. Such "experts" claim we'll have victory in helping our child overcome his fears if we try to explain why the thing he fears can't hurt him—or why he shouldn't worry even if the thing he fears *can* hurt him.

But the only answer to fear is obedience to and faith in the one true God. Anyone who teaches anything else doesn't know the answer and can only offer trivial and useless "methods"—lies disguised as "rational thinking."

Without faith in God, our usual response to fear on the part of our children is to be sympathetic. We try to put ourselves inside of our children's fears. We might even hope to dissuade their fears by letting them sleep with us or by looking through the drawers to assure them that no monsters live there. The worst response is when we ourselves become fearful about what our children fear, giving life to the fears and death to the faith of our children.

Our children don't need our well-intentioned efforts; they need *God*.

Of course, there are dangers that our children must learn to avoid, but we have to be very careful to avoid using ungodly fear as a teaching device, lest we teach them fear itself. If we are only to fear God, then teaching our children to fear anything else is teaching them to sin. We work against ourselves and God when we try to instill fears on the one hand even as we try to drive fears out on the other.

There *are* dangers this side of heaven, but the only fear that means anything is the fear of the Lord. Your child must be taught to fear disobeying God's commands in areas where the danger is under the child's control. And your child must be taught to let fears that are outside of his control drive him by faith into the arms of God.

David said: "I do not concern myself with great matters or things too wonderful for me. But I have stilled and quieted my soul" (Psalm 131:1-2). David had learned to fear and obey and have faith in his God. The result was— and still is for us today—a quiet soul.

Confidence Even When — the Teardrops Fall —

Many things make us shake and cry, but we must

learn to hold on to our confidence. The first step is to understand that we shed tears for two different reasons. The first reason is our own sinful folly. These are the self-inflicted wounds that come from not getting our own way, from anger and hatred, and from fear that comes from lack of faith. The second reason comes from outside ourselves, the tests and trials that come into all our lives. We must learn to deal with each of these in a totally different way.

When your children cry because of self-inflicted wounds (the result of selfishness, disobedience, cruelty, etc.), they *don't* need to be encouraged or receive a helping hand. Rather, they need a helping hand dropped on an appropriate target with accuracy and forcefulness. Parents have a built-in tendency to run to their children when they're crying or hurt, no matter the reason. Don't do it.

But then there are the true tears—tears that come because of the "Lonely Little Petunia in an Onion Patch" syndrome. You and your children, no matter how sweet you are to God, are living in a world of onions, and that is going to bring you tears. These "onions" can be things in the world or the church or even in your own past life that bring a godly sadness and tears, as they did to men like Nehemiah and Jeremiah and Jesus. They can also result from sadness at the loss of a loved one through death, or even from things that cause physical pain. These tears are appropriate and acceptable before God.

But the "onions" can also be tests and trials. One of the hardest things for a Christian to put into practice is the exhortation in James to "consider it pure joy... whenever you face trials of many kinds, *because you know that the testing of your faith develops perseverance*" (James 1:2-3). I know many Christians who can quote this passage, but how many of us really *do* it? How many of us live as though we really know that testing develops perseverance?

Our usual reaction to trials is to do anything *but* consider it pure joy. We cry and moan and doubt and ask God how He could let such a horrible thing happen to us.

And then we teach our children to do the same.

God doesn't want us to cry when He allows or brings a trial into our life. In fact, He *hates* it when we cry in the face of a trial. How do I know this? Because He commands us to "consider it pure joy." And if we don't, but start crying instead, we're disobeying God and He hates disobedience. He wants confidence, not complaints.

If Christians could really "consider it pure joy," no matter what, and teach their children to do the same, we would get the benefits of the promises of God that go with it. Everybody has trials. Christians can experience true peace and joy no matter the circumstances, and present a face and heart attitude to the world that would be awesome and irresistible.

Sometimes crying is appropriate; sometimes it isn't. Teach your children which is which. If you don't, I'll make a prediction.

Your children are going to make you cry.

Examine Your — *Confidence in Prayer* —

I once polled a group of high school and college students in a certain church on the subjects of the will of God and prayer. The highest percentage of time that anyone thought that he or she had known and been in the will of God was 20 percent. When asked what percentage of their prayers had been answered, they simply said that it was much less than that, and for some it was practically zero.

Why is this? How is this possible in churches that claim to believe in a personal and loving God? What's the use of talking about prayer and praying if our own children don't even believe that God is faithful enough to answer them clearly?

Folks, the problem of "unanswered" prayer is with *us*—not God. There are several reasons for our failed communication with the heavenly Father:

- Our lives are cluttered with worldly garbage and sin. God wouldn't and *couldn't* hear us, even if we could figure out what to ask Him. If you have sin in your heart, the only prayer He's interested in is a prayer of confession. If your children don't learn this, their prayer lives are doomed to failure.

- We pray for things that aren't in Scripture and don't pray for things that are. We don't take the time to find out what God has promised. We forget that "if we know that he hears us—whatever we ask—we know that we have what we asked of him" (1 John 5:15).

- We don't pray specifically enough or carefully enough. We shouldn't assume that just because God is all-knowing that He'll answer vague prayer.

- We pray without the primary motive of giving God the glory—both in our prayer and in the answer that we *know* will come (see James 4:3).

- We refuse to accept the conditions or obey the commands that go along with the promises. We want the prize without having to do our part—by *faith,* of course. God will not be mocked. He *expects* us to live by faith (See Mark 9:19). Jesus *couldn't* do miracles where there was no faith (see Mark 6:5-6).

- We really don't want just *any* answer. We usually have some idea of what we would like the answer to be, and then we tell God in our hearts that we'll accept any answer as long as it's the one we want. We have to remember that we can't hear if we aren't listening. And we can't hear the gentle voice of God if we are walking by sight.

Teach Your
— Children to Pray —

Teach your children to imagine a king. This king has just sent them a message that he'll answer any question they might have. He wants to relate to them in a personal way, but they have to remember that he's still a king and that they should go into his presence with a healthy amount of fear. Then ask your children this: How will you get ready for your time with the king?

With some encouragement on your part, they'll probably tell you that they would make sure they hadn't done anything to offend the king. They'd work on their question for a long time and leave out dumb questions. They'd make sure their question was clear and called for a clear answer. They'd see if the king had written anything on the subject of their question and then read it. They'd ask the king's messenger to guide them in the development and presentation of their question, and then wait for the right time.

If they're wise, they'll approach the king confidently but respectfully, and let him know that his answer— whatever it is—will be accepted at face value. Then they'll sit quietly until the king decides to answer, after they have thanked him for hearing them and, in advance, for answering their question. And finally, when they hear his answer, they'll go and do whatever he says. Show them that this will *always* bring favor from a king. And teach your children one more thing about this king: He is the King of kings.

— Sing in Prison —

Once, when I was standing up for something I believed in a very public and outspoken way, a man drove by in a car and yelled many gross insults at me. For once,

I responded in a godly way and wished him Godspeed and a good day.

I didn't think much about this until later, when I was sharing the importance of blessing your enemies with my then seven-year-old son Peter. As soon as I finished my first statement on the matter, he stopped my whole speech with a single comment, "I know that's what you're supposed to do. I saw you do it with that man."

Nothing has ever brought home to me more clearly the importance of living out the truths of God's Word— no matter how nonsensical they appear to our finely honed and doubtlessly infallible brain and emotions. God wants His people to do all kinds of things that just seem the opposite of logic and reason.

In this case, Jesus wants us to sing in man's prisons. He says:

> Blessed are you when men hate you, when they exclude you and insult you and reject your name as evil, because of the Son of Man. *Rejoice* in that day and leap for joy, because great is your reward in heaven. . . . Love your enemies, do good to those who hate you, bless those who curse you, pray for those who mistreat you. . . . Then your reward will be great, and *you will be sons of the Most High* (Luke 6:22-23,27-28,35).

So not only is this God's preferred response, but He also emphasizes that this will allow us to experience the fullness of being a son of God and bring us great reward. If these aren't three great reasons to rejoice and leap for joy, then there just aren't any. If you can teach this to your children, in an age of hating and cursing, you'll have opened up to them the exquisite possibility of countless blessings from God.

Be willing to expose your children—with you, at first—to attack from the world because of their stand for God. When you're attacked (see 2 Timothy 3:12), respond as Jesus commanded, and then rejoice and thank God that He has allowed you to suffer because of His name. There is more life-changing power in this course of action than any of us will ever be able to imagine, because supernatural responses get supernatural results.

For those of you who have never once been hated, excluded, insulted, rejected, cursed, or mistreated because of your life being lived for God in *this* world, rotten as this world is, I have only one question: What are you doing?

And someday, your children may have a second question for you: Where were you when God's people were being cursed?

Only one answer will satisfy your spirit as you look them in the eye.

"My child, I was singing in prison."

10

Balance

Fiction: Big mood swings are only natural.

Fact: The man who fears God will avoid all extremes (Ecclesiastes 7:18).

Does it seem sometimes as though your whole life is a struggle to find a balance between competing demands? That setting and holding the right priorities in the right order is even harder than balancing the family budget?

Man's struggle, both inside and outside of Christianity, is in many ways a struggle with the issue of balance. In fact, the reason man struggles is that he usually isn't very balanced. Man swings back and forth on a seldom-resting pendulum between talk of peace and merciless warfare, preaching tolerance and detesting difference, claiming unfailing love and gossiping about a loved one.

You probably feel the pull as a parent as well. From being too hard to being too soft, too interfering to too unavailable, too willing to share adult problems to too unwilling to share "embarrassing" truth, you can go back and forth in a frustrating cycle. One minute you can feel like a rock, and the next like mush. Without a balanced life, you'll be passing a heritage of imbalance and frustration along to your children.

You can stop the pendulum.

___ *Finding the Balance* ___

"Do not be overrighteous, neither be overwise—why destroy yourself?" These are not the words of a Buddhist or Hindu philosopher. These are flawless words from the mind of God, found in Ecclesiastes 7:16.

The Balance of God

What does this verse mean?

God is talking about balance. Scripture says, "Honest scales and balances are from the LORD; all the weights in the bag are of his making" (Proverbs 16:11). Our God is an absolutely balanced being, and this characteristic of balance is evident throughout His creation.

God asks these questions: "Who has measured the waters in the hollow of his hand, or with the breadth of his hand marked off the heavens? Who has held the dust of the earth in a basket, or weighed the mountains on the scales and the hills in a balance?" (Isaiah 40:12). God didn't just slap creation together; creation is totally precise.

This characteristic of balance is also clearly displayed in His fundamental relationship with man. Our God is balanced gloriously between justice and mercy. If He were an "extremist" on justice alone, this book wouldn't have been written. (I wouldn't be here.) If He were an "extremist" on mercy alone, no wrongs would ever be righted, the unrepentant wicked would not be punished, and faith or lack of faith in God would make no difference.

But God is perfectly balanced. *All* sin is justly punished. God is too just to overlook any sin, and too merciful not to provide a way out for those who cry out to Him in truth. Because of justice, each person is faced with damnation; because of mercy, each person is allowed the choice to be forgiven and accept God's grace by faith.

God is a God of balance, and in the verse that opened this section He is telling us something about balance. But what?

He is simply trying to tell us to be like Him—to be balanced. He says in His Word, "Love and faithfulness meet together; righteousness and peace kiss each other" (Psalm 85:10). He wants us to love people, but never at the expense of faithfulness to His truth. He wants us to mix righteousness with understanding, mercy, and peace, and knowledge with gentleness, humility, and sensitivity. He wants us to stand out, in the same way His Son stood out while He walked upon the earth.

Imagine how tempted Jesus must have been to wipe out the sinful cesspool in which He found Himself, and yet He wept over Jerusalem and sought fellowship with those much less perfect than Him. Can you understand His being able to condemn people for their hardness of heart even as He was preparing to die for them?

He could do it because He had balance.

Even in His two comings we can see His balance. His first coming was not "to condemn the world, but to save the world" (John 3:17). But in His second coming, "With justice he judges and makes war" (Revelation 19:11). He's the Savior of those under judgment and the Judge of those who will not choose to be saved.

Finding Balance Through the Scriptures

So what is this thing called *balance*?

Balance isn't compromise. Compromise is agreeing to combine what you know to be right with what you know to be wrong. Balance is combining two things which you know are right. Balance isn't compartmentalizing your spirit so that you can deal with gross contradictions; this schizophrenic thinking is a refusal to acknowledge that there is absolute truth. Balance is an acknowledgment that absolute truth cannot be refused.

And balance is not another word for complacency or apathy or "conservatism." Balance in your spirit is not an excuse to avoid being radical, but rather it *calls* for being radical—"proceeding from the root . . . fundamental; reaching to the center or ultimate source." Teach your children to be like God—to be balanced. They should try to understand all of God's truth on a particular subject and then believe and apply it with zeal. Balance is so apparent in God's Word that an honest search of the Bible will produce people of balance.

For example, Scripture tells us to "speak up for those who cannot speak for themselves" (Proverbs 31:8). This would certainly apply to unborn babies facing an abortionist, a handicapped baby facing a conspiracy to starve him to death, and a helpless elderly person facing the non-treatment, passive euthanasia of our burden-eliminating medical professionals. God tells us to be watchmen and warn those who are fighting against Him.

But at the same time Scripture tells us to "go and make disciples of all nations . . . teaching them to obey everything I have commanded you" (Matthew 28:19-20). He adds to this that we also should be willing to forgive time after time (Matthew 18:21-22).

So what do we do as we look at these Scriptures, and others, with regard to our culture's great disrespect for human life?

We should teach our children to do *all* of these things, in balance. They should be taught to speak up and work for the helpless, and to warn those who are attacking the helpless that they're wrong and will be judged. But they also should be taught that they're responsible to hold out the gift of eternal life to any of these people who will listen, and to be willing to instantly forgive those who seek forgiveness and to leave those who are unrepentant to the balanced and perfect judgment of God.

In short, our children should be taught that they have been commanded and empowered by God to stand up for those who can't stand on their own, and then to leave the results and any required judging in the hands of the Lord.

And what about imbalance? God reduces the results of imbalance to a simple question: "Why destroy yourself?" With that sobering thought in mind, I would like to ask a parallel question: Why destroy your child? Find the balance.

___ *Separate or Salt?* ___

A question that constantly circulates through serious families and bodies of believers is this: Should we be separate from the world, or should we be salt?

The answer is yes.

We should be separate and we should be salt. To some, this might seem like a contradiction, but it isn't a contradiction at all. It *appears* contradictory because of three failures in our understanding, the first two of which were discussed in detail in the preceding section:

- We fail to understand God's basic principle of balance. From the delicate balance of the universe to that of the atom, from riches to poverty, from being "overrighteous" to "overwicked," God's creation is always to be balanced between unscriptural extremes.

- We fail to understand the difference between *balance* and *compromise*. Balance is spiritual level-heartedness that follows *all* of God's Word, not just part of it. Compromise is thinking God's Word in your head and living the world in your life.

- We fail to understand that one (to separate) is a prerequisite of the other (to salt). With children, this means that we must put them in a "greenhouse" and enable them to become salt. We can't afford to expose them to worldly influences too soon. With adults, it means that without the separation—of attitudes, of beliefs and actions, and of simple time away with the Lord—our salt shakers will be empty.

So we must do both: We and our children must separate first and salt later. We must first be people of prayer and meditation and conviction, and then people of action and influence and persuasion. We must train our children for proper responses in their early years, and then gradually expose them to opportunities to respond as they grow older.

The *Random House Encyclopedia* says, "Salt has been used as a preservative for thousands of years. It extends the storage life of foods by inhibiting the growth of bacteria. Salt and spices are both used to make food more palatable, *especially if it has already begun to deteriorate*".

There is no question that our culture has already begun to deteriorate. Decay is proceeding at breakneck speed in our "enlightened" culture. But we can surely preserve and make others' lives more palatable by being salt. Without question, we can extend the storage life of Western civilization if we and our children will pour ourselves generously on this gray, smelly, tasteless society in which we live.

But just as salt is only useful when it's been separated from the earth and is fresh and pure, so our effectiveness depends on our separation from the world. We and our children must have such an intimate relationship with our heavenly Father that we can be used to bring out the flavor of a feast, instead of being good for nothing "except to be thrown out and trampled by men" (Matthew 5:13).

God tells us that we are to "be merciful to those who doubt; snatch others from the fire and save them; to others show mercy, *mixed with fear—hating even the clothing stained by corrupted flesh*" (Jude 22-23). We are to salt the earth, never forgetting for a minute our fear of God and our hatred of evil. Jesus could rub elbows with sinners without getting His arms dirty because He was

God in the flesh, because He spent 30 years preparing for His salting ministry, and because of solitary times with His Father after the ministry had begun.

Pass the salt, please.

__ *Resisters and Adapters* __

All of us and all of our children have desires to resist some things and to adapt to others. Some of us are so resistant to so many things that resistance becomes a way of life, while others are so able to blend into any landscape that even a chameleon would recognize them as a brother. Here, too, we must find God's balance.

There are three key questions to ask when considering the balance between resisting and adapting in yourself and in your children:

1. Is this person usually resisting outside input or is he adapting to it?

2. What kinds of things should he be resisting or adapting to?

3. How do I get him to resist and adapt to the right things?

Those who resist most of the time usually take heart from Thoreau's motto: "Any fool can make a rule, and every fool will mind it." Their first question is usually, "Why?"—not the inquisitive "Why?" of most small children, but the "you had better have a good reason" form of the question. They hear the different drumbeat loud and clear and hate the parental trumpet blast that, to them, often seems out of rhythm and out of tune. This young person, however, is a potential man of faith in skunk's clothing. If *you* can resist the natural desire to crush this resistance, the body of Christ might have itself another David.

Those who adapt most of the time have a motto of their own: "Every fool can break a rule, but I'm no fool; I'll mind it." Their first question is usually, "Why me?"— whether they're being forced by parents to resist when resistance is uncomfortable or forced by peers to adapt to things which are offensive. They hear a flute playing a gentle melody and usually try to keep themselves in harmony with those around them. This young person, however, is a potential man of faith in sheep's clothing. If *you* can resist the natural desire to force him to stand up for himself, the body of Christ might have itself another Abraham.

It's your responsibility to teach each of these bright spirits the importance of resisting or adapting to the right things. There really is "a time to plant and a time to uproot" (Ecclesiastes 3:2). We have to uproot (or keep from rooting in the first place) the mind of humanism, the counsel of the wicked, and the walk by sight. At the same time, we must plant the mind of Jesus, the ways of the wise, and the walk of faith.

Balance isn't compromise. Compromise is agreeing to combine what you know to be right with what you know to be wrong. Balance is combining two things which you know are right.

One of the areas we have worked on with our children is the matter of principles versus practices. We have shown them the difference between these things from a biblical perspective. We have taught them to resist strongly the challenges to their principles, but to adapt and be flexible with regard to their practices (see 1 Corinthians 9:22), and even to delight in these differences. It is all too easy to fold on our principles while we fight to the death for our self-sanctified preferences.

Those who resist God's way must be taught to adapt, not by sheer willpower and force, but by the power of example. Proverbs says: "He who heeds discipline shows the way to life, but whoever ignores correction leads others astray" (10:17). The force method is dangerous as well as ineffective, although it might seem to work for a time. However, the rebellion continues to grow, and now under great pressure that will explode when the child is older. He may then dedicate his powerful will to the resistance of all that you supposedly stand for.

Simply stated: Your discipline of your children had better be totally in line with your discipline of yourself.

It should be no real surprise that those who are adapting to the world's way should be taught resistance in the same way. The method of forcing them to resist will not be effective in producing persons who are mighty in spirit. It will either produce a confirmed adapter who *looks* like a leader but is really leading others in conformity, or a rebellious person who will resist everything *you* say and adapt like putty in the hands of his friends. One is a facade and the other is a monster.

This is not an argument in favor of growing little revolutionaries who will glare in your eye and spit in your face whenever you say, "Do this." But there comes a time when the money changers must be driven from the temple, and only a godly resister can do it.

Follow Nehemiah's Example

If you're looking for a role model of the balanced life between resisting and adapting, look to Nehemiah.

As a resister, he hated what he saw, and wept over the evil and what it had done; he went personally into the effort and counted the cost; he explained the situation to those who would be doing the work; he despised and pushed aside the abuse of the strong men who opposed God; and he encouraged the people until God's wall was rebuilt.

As an adapter, however, he stayed under the authority of God and the king; he kept his knowledge to himself until he himself was ready to act; he trusted all judgment to God; and he didn't lord it over the people.

Nehemiah could dismiss any notion of dominating the people by saying, "Out of reverence for God I did not act like that. Instead, I devoted myself to the work" (Nehemiah 5:15-16). The result: a successful project with resistance against resistance, followed by a meeting where "all the people assembled as one man. . . . From the days of Joshua son of Nun until that day, the Israelites had not celebrated it like this. And their joy was very great" (Nehemiah 8:1,17).

— *Majoring on the Minor* —

You only have so many years, so many days, so many hours to spend on the development of your child.

Don't spend them majoring on the minor.

Scripture is very clear that each of us has a significant part to play in his time and place as God's plan unfolds. Satan, of course, is aware of this, too. And one of Satan's most devious schemes, improved upon by millennia of practice, is to throw us a *red herring*.

What is a satanic red herring?

It isn't seafood, believe me. A satanic red herring is something he gives us in the hellish hope that we'll spend an inordinate amount of time pursuing the thing beyond all bounds of reason. Since he's kept his angel-of-light costume, he picks items that seem to be worthwhile to pursue. We then spend our time hounding our children to death to comply with virtually worthless rules.

The effects of this are devastating. We stop spending time on the really important things, leaving our children in a spiritual vacuum. We get frustrated because the trivial can never be quite up to our standards. Our children start spending their best efforts to comply with our demands, which teaches *them* to major on the minor. All the while, the possibilities of affecting life in a powerful way evaporate. Our children learn to grease the squeaky wheel. They will finally rebel against this terrific on-slaught of triviality, probably after they are old enough to make their rebellion stick.

To list these red herrings is impossible because even Satan is creative. You'll have to ferret them out by asking yourself questions: Is this really important? If he doesn't learn this, will it leave him with a flaw in his character? Does doing this have eternal value? Is not doing it a sin against God? Does God care about this? When some-thing really bugs you, come back to this section and ask yourself these questions—before you launch your attack.

Nagging is usually a sign that the trivial is in action. If it were important, you wouldn't nag; you would *insist*. If you find yourself nagging, ask yourself this question: Is this worth taking a stand on? If it is, stop nagging and start standing. If it isn't, stop nagging and sit down.

One final note on a clever twist that Satan can put on a red herring: When someone else is doing a little major-ing on the minor, Satan can get you to respond in kind. I know some parents who rightly rejected a Christian school's overemphasis on things like hair length, and then responded by dramatically withdrawing themselves from even *considering* such a school for their children.

What starts out as a stand against the trivial can become merely a trivial stand. We can pride ourselves on being free of this disease when we are in fact living it out in front of our children. And they'll learn the terrible lesson that it's valuable to enter their spirits in a battle against the valueless.

This is not to say that we are to let minor offenses slip by when they're offenses of *principle*. On these we should take a stand, for two reasons. First, because these minor offenses will grow into major ones pretty quickly. And second, because violations of principle are despicable to God even if they are small.

So many minor things can swallow up our precious years. Even as Christians, we can spend our time on this planet in an entirely insignificant way. Too many children today—and since they will be the parents of the next generation, it will probably be true tomorrow—are being immersed in the insignificant by their parents.

This is perhaps the greatest damage that majoring on the minor can produce. It leaves no time to do anything but minor on the major. It causes us to make the same mistake as the Jewish leaders of Jesus' day, who watched the Lord of glory, the object of their hope, with envy and hatred to see if He would break some minor and over-emphasized rule. They majored on the minor and, as a result, minored on the major question of their lives.

I wonder how many parents, when they're standing before the Lord, will tremble when they hear Jesus' questions about why they didn't teach their children principles and help them to live by them. Will their only answer be a pathetic, "But, Lord, I was too busy trying to get them to eat their turnips"?

Listen, if he won't clean his plate or button his coat or go right to sleep or stay out of the mud or sing out during the Christmas program, then know this very major thing: *It's no big deal.*

___ Seasons of Life ___

Life is not always the same. Every family's life goes through stages or seasons (see Ecclesiastes 3:1-8). You must ask God to show you what season of life you are in, and then seek to find the balance in that season. For example, if you have four children under five years old, you should have a different mix of inside and outside activities than if your children are young adults. Don't be embarrassed or feel guilty about making necessary adjustments—for a season.

Part 3

Carrying Out the Plan

11

Helping and Hurting Your Vision

Fiction: As parents, we just have to hope for the best.

Fact: Where there is no vision, the people are unrestrained, but happy is he who keeps the law (Proverbs 29:18, NASB).

In this chapter, we're going to look first at nine ideas that can help you advance your vision as a parent, and then nine ideas that can point you in the wrong direction.

Are you committed to carrying out the plan of proactive parenting? Then don't just *read* this chapter. Stop after each item and ask yourself how this concept can be built into your life and your parenting. When you've finished, go back over each heading and make a mark by the one you want to start on this week. Then, with God's help, put that one into practice.

1. Learn to Be a Pilgrim

A *pilgrim* is defined by Webster as "one who travels to some holy place." Parent, are you a pilgrim?

You're not traveling to *some* holy place; you're traveling to *the* holy place. Or at least that's what you're supposed to be doing (see Hebrews 11:13-14). Are you a devotee—one whose entire life and walk is dedicated to the goal of arriving at the holy place spiritually intact? Or are you clinging to your "fire insurance" while you sink your roots into this barren, dying world?

We must be careful what we talk about and set our hearts on. I know of one Christian family who spent most of their meal times and other conversation times talking about possessions—gadgets, trinkets, *things*. Their oldest child is now working on his third marriage and has immersed his whole life in things. They missed the deep truth of 2 Corinthians 4:18, Hebrews 11:16, and Psalm 84:5-7,10.

We should do all we can to reconstruct this place we are traveling through, while at the same time remembering that the only thing of lasting interest here is the other pilgrims in the tents next to yours—and those who might want to join the journey.

Think like a pilgrim. You'll be pleased with the results.

2. Learn Who Your Best Neighbor Is

The literal translation of John 1:14 is delightful: "The Word became flesh and *pitched his tent among us.*" Jesus Himself came and lived here with us as a pilgrim; His tent is right next to yours.

Never let your children forget one crucial fact: Our faith is ultimately in a person, not just in things that speak of the person. In all things, the Word of God stands, but there is no magic in the words themselves. Many have read them and remained unsaved or powerless. The one who reads these words must encounter the One who wrote the Book.

I remember two sisters who had memorized more Scripture than almost anyone I've ever known. They had correct answers to almost every question, and they could beat any well-trained adult in a "sword drill" every time. But I never knew two more prideful, obnoxious, nasty young people. They knew something—but not Someone.

> *Never let your children forget one crucial fact: Our faith is ultimately in a person, not just in things that speak of the person.*

Nobody knew more about the Scriptures than the scribes and Pharisees, who killed the One about whom the Book was written (see John 5:39-40). It's immeasurably more valuable to know only one promise or command and to believe and act upon it, than to know a thousand of them without believing one (see Philippians 3:16).

Let's work hard to teach our kids to meet with Jesus, and to show them that the Bible is important because its author is alive, watching, judging, saving, loving—and coming again.

3. Learn to Sacrifice

What is worship? "Therefore, I urge you, brothers, in view of God's mercy to offer your bodies as living sacrifices, holy and pleasing to God—*this is your spiritual worship*" (Romans 12:1).

What? You thought that worship was praising God in word and song? Enjoying a choir explode with power on a beautiful hymn? Lifting your hands and dancing before the Lord? Nope. These things can overflow from a worshipful *life*, but they themselves aren't worship. We have worship *meetings*, when we should be having meetings for worship *people*. And calling meetings full of non-sacrificing, unholy, and unpleasing people "worship" is biblically inaccurate (see Malachi 2:3).

Let your children see you give your time when you're tired, your money when you'd like to buy something for yourself, your convenience when somebody you really don't like asks you for help. Urge your children to use their money to buy food for the poor, help an elderly neighbor, or work on a project with a younger child. I remember how I felt when my oldest son gave up several free days to help build a new classroom at his school.

Sacrifice. It defines worship. It *is* worship. Lives lived out in a sacrificial way always catch our attention. As your children do something sacrificial, you'll know with certainty that you're parenting true worshipers. Give them a big hug and praise God in their presence for their sacrificial lives.

Now *that's* a worship meeting.

4. *Learn That You're Not the Only One*

You believe that you are the sole guardian of your children's spirits and welfare; that you alone must protect them from outside influences; that no one else has the right to instruct or discipline your children. You believe that you're truly the only one—outside of God— destined to be a source of wisdom and acceptable as a model for their developing spirits.

And you are wrong.

Many things can contribute to this attitude: insecurity about our own beliefs; lack of closeness to others, so we're uncertain about what they might believe or do; or just plain old pride—the idea that somehow we are *it*, and anyone else is second best. The fruit won't be good. This approach will teach kids to resent and reject and rebel against other authority. Your critical words about other authorities will only add to the effect.

I heard one man in a Bible study tell the others in strong language, "No one other than me had better ever correct my children." Not so surprisingly, people avoided his children. Also, not so surprisingly, his children were out of control. He didn't see it, and no one wanted to incur his criticism, disdain, or wrath.

Your children can be incredibly blessed by others, and you can get insights about your children from others with different perspectives and spiritual gifts than yours.

Don't push these godly helpers away—even the slightest resistance on your part can stop them cold. Even if they're *convicted* about helping, they won't do it because of their fear of alienating or offending you. "Too bad, so sad," as my son Peter used to say.

God is the primary influence, and the rest of us are just His tiny helpers. You are an important one.

But you're not the only one.

5. Learn to Grovel

Although most parents might not realize it, groveling is one of their most critical activities.

The Bible says that "he who walks with the wise grows wise" (Proverbs 13:20). We and our children need wise people who care about us and who will spend truly valuable time with us. Immersion in Christian activity is fine, but it is not a substitute for walking with godly mentors. What your children need is an intimate relationship with a few outstanding men or women (probably not peers) who will dedicate their *lives*, and not just their time, to your children.

I decided to invest myself in a young woman, with the full support and encouragement of her parents. She listened to what I shared with her about God and life, and she flourished in part because I was able to give her the truth packaged in care and relationship. Her family moved far away and we lost touch, but years later her father told me about her husband. "We really like him," he said. "And we're not surprised that he reminds us of you." What an encouragement to invest in others!

Wise people won't be easy to find, and the best choices may also be the busiest people. So what are you going to do when you find one? *Grovel.* To grovel is "to humble oneself; to lie or crawl with the face downward, as in abject humility." Plead with these potential spirit builders to invest themselves in your children. Don't take "no" for an answer. You want godly children, and you'll seek and find and encourage and support those few who can help you get there.

Once you're on your knees, the rest is easy.

6. *Learn to Whisper*

Whispering may be one of the most important things you can do as a parent.

God didn't speak to Elijah in the wind, earthquake, or fire. He spoke in a "gentle whisper" (see 1 Kings 19:11-12). Many parents, though, appear to their children to be more like wind, earthquake, and fire. We act as though parenting, to be effective, has to be *loud*. God isn't like that. So why are we? How would we like it if God yelled out in our next church meeting, "Hey you! Would you mind getting your mouth under control?" We would be totally humiliated, and more likely to resent God than to follow Him.

I began to apply this with my own children, many years ago, when they were misbehaving. I either went to them or quietly asked them to come to me, and I whispered in those little ears what I wanted them to know. I was amazed at how my correction went over a hundred times better than the old earthquake approach. They were really listening to me, rather than resenting my open disrespect.

The golden rule (see Matthew 7:12) applies here. You don't like vocal correction in front of others, and neither do your children. Correct them, but treat them with the dignity that God—who doesn't broadcast *your* follies in public—intended them to have. You can turn a big potential lemon into a cold glass of lemonade, if you will do with them what God does with you.

Just whisper.

7. Learn to Test with Praise

What's the best way to tell if your children are developing any character to go along with their skills and abilities? "The crucible for silver and the furnace for gold, but man is tested by the praise he receives" (Proverbs 27:21).

Watch for these telltale signs of trouble:

- Do your children do things primarily to receive praise?
- Do they actively seek and solicit praise (see Proverbs 25:27)?
- Do they praise themselves (see Proverbs 30:32)?
- Do they forget to be "completely humble and gentle" (Ephesians 4:2)?
- Do they answer praise with questions that sound humble but are really efforts to secure more praise?

How should praise be answered? Thoughtfully, outwardly, and upwardly. Thoughtfully, because you want your children to be able to discern the difference between real praise and flattery (see Proverbs 29:5). Outwardly, because you want them to be gracious and encouraging to the one who is praising them. And upwardly, because you don't want them to be fools who cling to praise (see Proverbs 26:8) when all praise ultimately belongs to God anyway (see Isaiah 26:12).

You must praise your children. They need it from you; they need their "pride" (see Proverbs 17:6) to encourage them in good directions. And you need to see their response, so you'll know what's in their hearts.

Let the test begin.

8. Learn to Have Family Nights

If you aren't dedicating at least one night or special time a week to the spiritual development of your family

as a family, you shouldn't be surprised to find out someday that you aren't a real family at all.

The idea of a family as a refuge is being eroded by the
attitude that living in the same building makes a group
of people a family. Many families today don't even take
one meal together on a daily basis. These everyday
regrouping times are vital in keeping a family connected. Make at least one of them into an extended time
of joy around the Lord, doing things like:

- Have a special meal or dessert, and spend time
  "dissecting" life together. Try to draw everyone
  into the conversation.
- Read Scripture, and then draw individual pictures
  to describe what impressed you. Share the pictures with each other.
- Work on a longer-term project (oil painting, plaque,
  etc.).
- Play a store-bought or homemade Bible game.
- Sing, with each one picking out a song on a rotat-
  ing basis.
- Listen to tapes of Bible stories or music.
- Do a project for someone else (a meal for a shut-in,
  yard work for Grandpa, etc.).
- Take a Scripture and put it into practice (for example, sell a possession and give the money to the
  poor).
- Eat out, if the funds are there. Share with each
  other openly. Who knows who might be listening?

Fight like crazy to keep this in your schedule, and
work to keep it consistent and fresh. Many things will
try to squeeze it out.

Treat these things like a contagious disease.

9. *Learn to Create Memory Pockets*

Think back to your own childhood. There are probably at least a few special or gentle pictures that will come

to mind and heart. Take a minute to quietly remember those soft times. Where have these paintings been kept all these years? In memory pockets.

My father worked seven days a week and had little time for me. But even so, I remember a wonderful day when he took me to a park. We sat on a hill and watched a construction crew finish paving the street in front of us. I don't remember anything we said, but that memory lives on, full of goodness and quietness, a lifelong moment of closeness and belongingness. Your own parenting will live in memories far beyond your time on earth as well. It takes three things to make a good memory pocket: time, love, and softness.

We can also make bad memory pockets, full of cruelty, hate, tongue-lashings, and broken promises. Nightmares can take up all of the space where joy alone should be. You don't want to be remembered like this. You can stay away from this by the power of God, and give your children the things of Philippians 4:8 to think on instead. Start stuffing, with God's help.

And fill up those tiny pockets with fistfuls of joy.

Fiction: So you make a few mistakes. Big deal. Nobody's perfect until they get to heaven.

Fact: Let us throw off everything that hinders (Hebrews 12:1).

Just as there are at least nine things that can advance your vision as a parent, there are at least nine things that will make your mission more difficult. Let's take a look at them.

1. Make Your Child a Clone of You

It's appropriate that you encourage your children to become like you—but not *exactly* like you.

Each child is a physical and spiritual package that's absolutely unique. He should be treated like the treasure he is and respected for his magnificent design. We want to impress the principles we live by on this child, but we should let these principles take special form in this one-of-a-kind creation.

Although my oldest son and I share a common set of principles and ways of looking at life, our personalities and interests and abilities are very different. He is artistically gifted while I work for hours to perfect stick figures. He is mechanically inclined while I need my wife to open medicine bottles. He has a great ability to say funny things while I have to work not to say things funny. We're united in spirit, diverse in gifts.

We're the same, but different. We can each affect people who would be untouched by just one of us and a clone. God has an all-original cast—unique people, planned for specific times and places, to make a dramatic difference for Him. Get excited about helping your child discover all the things that make him special. There has never been another exactly like him, and there never will be again. Help your child to be what God wants him to be, and not just a carbon copy of you.

Besides, hasn't *one* of you already tried God's patience enough?

2. Be the Bland Leading the Bland

Have you ever noticed how easy it is to fill up your days with "stuff"?

Activities, while fine if kept in perspective, can take the place of thought and creativity. Our children can then pick up this empty way of life. We settle for so little when there is so much to have. We can be potentially everything but practically nothing. We can teach our children to miss the glory of a life sold out to God by the example of our own lives which are lived without expectation from God or enthusiasm for God. For this, we most certainly deserve to be sent to our room.

God stoops down to make us great.
Great—that's what God's talking about.
Getting by—that's what we too easily
talk about.

One man I knew did everything with rich enthusiasm. It was as though he had just come from the throne room of God and was full of excitement about what he had seen. He sang with more gusto and meaning than I've ever heard from a man, before or since. I used to try to sit in front of him in church because having him sing in my ears was so encouraging. Would it surprise you if I said that his four children all drip with excitement about God?

God stoops down to make us great (see Psalm 18:35). *Great*—that's what God's talking about. *Getting by*—that's what we too easily talk about. Force yourself, with God's help, to be interested in His agenda. Ask: Why me? Why now? Why here? God will give you the answers (see Jeremiah 33:3), if only you'll ask. Ultimately, there's nothing more exciting than God.

Let the children see it in you, and then watch them shine.

3. Abuse Your Child's Spirit

Just as there are many ways to be dead, there are many ways to be abused. Some hurt worse than others and leave deeper scars.

Physical and sexual abuse are horrors beyond words. Such destruction wrought upon helpless little spirits leaves scars and damage that can affect their ability to relate to others for a lifetime. If you are this kind of abuser, you need to stop reading and get on your knees before God (see James 4:7-10). Then find someone who can help you work through this ugly thing.

But spiritual abuse, the demolition of a little spirit by omission of spiritual things or by words of hate and anger, can also bring condemnation down on your head (see Mark 9:42).

Ken was a Christian who boiled over at the slightest thing that didn't go his way. He would rage at his wife over dishes, laundry, disorganization, timeliness of meals, and the whereabouts of things he himself had misplaced. His assaults on his children, who were even less able to defend themselves, were reckless, cruel, and unpredictable. When I confronted him on this, he told me that he was just being "honest," that he just had a different "personality," that he was simply being "authoritative," and that he was a "normal" dad. This "normal" dad's children, however, saw it differently. They viewed him with loathing as a hard, cold man.

We can spiritually abuse our children in a number of ways: neglecting spiritual things in the home; feeding their bodies while starving their spirits; requiring their participation in deadening meetings in church; placing them in a bad school (whether it's a "Christian" school or not); and, of course, destroying them with your own angry, mean words. To sum up: Don't abuse your children's spirits.

And don't let anyone else do it, either.

4. Pick a Formula and Pigeonhole Your Child

I have a confession to make: *I'm a wintry, right-brained, first-born, strong-willed, irregular choleric.* There you have it. I'm glad it's out.

We live in an age of generalizations and categorizations. And there's nothing wrong with this if they have some truth-related value that helps us understand life and the world around us.

But what if they only *sound* true? We tend too easily to latch on to the "rule of thumb," the shortcut, the quick-fix way of dealing with problems, the clever analysis that converts a full spiritual meal into bite-sized chunks. These unwarranted generalizations have several attributes in common:

- They deal with outward appearance (see Galatians 2:6).

- They can lead to prejudice—preconceived ideas in your dealings with your children (see 2 Corinthians 5:16).

- They can confuse your parenting and lead to self-fulfilling prophecies. Your children become what you've thought them to be.

- They can lead you to "explain," but not meet or solve, your children's legitimate needs, problems, or sins.

- They can substitute for intimacy and prevent you from getting to know your children's immortal inner being.

- They can cause you to wrongly differentiate between people (see Galatians 3:28).

We can listen to these theories and end up agreeing, laughing, and then, horror of horrors, putting them into practice. But God has already done all of the categorizing necessary. There are the sons of God and the sons of the devil. There are the sheep and there are the goats. There are the faithful and there are the unfaithful. The truth is, we all started out as wintry, no-brained, once-born/twice dead, strong-willed, irregular, temperamental people. Don't categorize your children. Instead, give them the opportunity to be in the only category that counts: the redeemed.

5. Hide Out in the Christian Ghetto

In society there is a force operating on the Christian community that says if we are to be tolerated at all, we must be roped off and isolated from having any effect on anyone or anything else. We can have our beliefs as long as we don't impose them on others. We are different, strange, a threat to the environment which secular man has worked so hard to build (see John 11:47-48). And so we have been rounded up and stuffed into the Christian ghetto.

But I know a few people who are still going about their *Father's* business. Regardless of society, they are invading and pervading every area of life—and reclaiming it all for Him. My friends Richard and Carol believe that *all* of life should operate on Kingdom principles, that God's Word is all true and has all of the necessary answers, and that no legitimate area of life is off-limits to a child of God. They pray against strongholds. They are involved in politics. They fight when others quit. They won't cooperate. They won't stay in the ghetto.

Eliminate from your family's vocabulary phrases like "full-time Christian work," as though there's any other kind! We need to teach our children to be totally committed to God, to be effective "out there" where the war is going on, to exercise authority over a creation that Jesus has already redeemed.

Either that, or our children will die—in the ghetto.

6. Nurture Your Own Blind Spots

It's amazing to me how many parents think that their children are perfect, right up to the moment that they can't understand them at all.

The easiest person to fool is always ourselves. We *want* to believe the best about our children. Satan can use deceit and treachery to develop major blind spots which prevent us from seeing our children's folly. We listen to those who flatter our parenting abilities or know us too superficially to see the real problems, even as we wall out other Christians who might be able to help.

Our excuses are many:

- "He's just a little boy. He'll settle down later on."
- "What can you expect from a child?"
- "They just don't know her like I do."
- "With all due respect, she's none of your business."
- "He might be a little rough, but he's basically a good boy."

The only way to avoid this malady is to look clearly, with others' help, at the spirits of our little ones. Don't excuse rotten behavior at all. Call a skunk a skunk. Dig deeply into their hearts so that you can see the dirty parts that you *know* are there (see Romans 3:23). And then help them take the dirt to Christ.

I guarantee it beats sweeping it under the carpet.

7. *Allow Complaining in Your Home*

Moslems are careful not to complain about the weather, for fear that they will offend the One who sent it. Christians should be so careful.

We have to teach our children to never complain about anything received from the hand of God. We have to teach them by our own example, as well as by making complaining off limits in their lives. With God's help, we can show them how to really practice Philippians 4:6 and receive the peace promised in the following verses.

In our home, we have a simple practice that reminds us about the Bible's stand against complaining: If you complain, you get more of what you *don't* want and less of what you *do*. If I tell the kids at 7 P.M. that bedtime is 8 P.M. and they complain, I tell them bedtime is now 7:45. If they complain again, we go to 7:30, and so on. If they complain *at* 8, they go to bed early the next night. If they complain about a certain food, that's all they get for a meal or two. Children practice discomfort avoidance; they'll usually come around quickly.

We try not to complain in our house for three simple reasons: First, God tells us not to (see Philippians 2:14), which is sufficient; second, we don't want to miss anything from the Lord, or get more of what we don't want and less of what we do; and third, we are wisely fearful, and don't want to offend anyone that powerful (see Psalm 90:11; 1 Corinthians 10:10-11). The choice appears simple: complaints or peace.

Be different. Choose peace.

8. Never Forget a Grudge

Although Scripture makes room for us to hate *God's* enemies (see Psalm 139:21-22), it's too easy to miss that truth while we rage in our heart against some long-ago wrong.

God has no room for petty grudges, and He wants us to let them go. "If he sins against you seven times a day, and seven times comes back to you and says, 'I repent,' forgive him," Jesus said (Luke 17:4). This is an amazing thing. It's why "the apostles said to the Lord, 'Increase our faith!'" (verse 5).

If someone has wronged your child, hurt him, insulted or embarrassed him, you have a golden opportunity. Teach your child how to pray God's blessing on this "enemy," and pray together for him. Help your child make or buy something for the other child, send him nice notes and cards, invite him along on a family outing. It'll probably blow the other child's socks off. If the situation arises in your own life, you can do the same and set a terrific example.

Why do this? Because God, remarkably, is kind to the ungrateful and wicked (see Luke 6:35). You and I are living proof. And if we do the same for others, we will be like God, receive great reward, and be true sons of the

Most High. Along with not burning your hand, these are some pretty outstanding reasons not to hold a grudge.

9. *Don't Take Full Responsibility for Your Failures*

It's appropriate that, in our modern age of rapidly increasing failure accompanied by rapidly decreasing responsibility, we would see the introduction of "no-fault" parenthood.

It goes something like this. You give parenting your best shot. You think you've hit a home run, and then your child turns out to be more like Attila the Hun than your lovely Aunt Rose. You analyze it carefully and determine that you couldn't have done any better, that it's really nobody's fault, and now you can go on hoping that she will solve her problem, *wherever* it came from.

I often hear this comment: "You know, they're such great people. I don't know *what* could have happened to their family!" But children don't come out of a box of Wheaties. Actions have consequences. Inaction has consequences. *Everything* has consequences. A child's behavior doesn't come from *nowhere*. For better or worse, the main thing that "happens" to a family is *you*.

This is why God can absolutely insist that no man can be a leader in a church unless he has children who are true believers, who obey not just out of force but with proper respect, and who cannot be accused of disobedience (see 1 Timothy 3:1-13; Titus 1:6-9). Otherwise, a leader *must* step down. How would this be a reasonable qualification if the results of parenting weren't under a father's control?

The antidote for "don't blame me" parenting is a "take the beach" attitude. The enemy is fighting to hold onto your child's heart. But with God's help, you can invade this precious territory. Get a foothold, and then slug it out with blood, sweat, and tears, bullets flying over your head, your eye always on the mountain of victory that awaits you. If you've already lost ground, recognize it, repent of it, ask God and your child for forgiveness, and press on! (See Philippians 3:12-14.) You can take responsibility, even in the face of past failures. And you can win.

12

Education and Schooling

Fiction: You've got to get an education to get ahead.

Fact: Let not the wise man boast of his wisdom ... but let him who boasts boast about this: that he understands and knows me, that I am the LORD (Jeremiah 9:23a,24a).

Education and schooling is often an area of great consternation for Christian parents. Which option is best? Public school, private school, Christian school, home school? Are several of these good choices, at different stages of a child's development? Should Christian children be witnesses in the public school? What if there aren't any good Christian schools? What if I don't have the money for anything but public school?

In the first place, the Bible doesn't talk about *education* and *schooling*, but rather about *instruction* and *discipling*. It tells us we should train ourselves "to be godly" (1 Timothy 4:7), for our own success as well as our children's.

Formal education *can* be the way to a job and material success, and it can even be a tool to help our children achieve success in the really important things. But it is only a tool, and we, as parents, must keep control of the tool because God holds us responsible. We have to understand that schooling is not the critical thing for success with God.

Perhaps Mark Twain had it right when he said, "I never let schooling interfere with my education."

The purpose of education is to shape the character of our children. Samuel Johnson believed this was at the heart of true education: "The supreme end of education is expert discernment in all things—the power to tell the good from the bad, the genuine from the counterfeit, and to prefer the good and the genuine to the bad and the counterfeit." (See also Hebrews 5:14.)

Making decisions regarding a child's education is tough. I'd like to help you think clearly about the potential advantages and disadvantages of each form of schooling, so I've listed them for you, school-type by school-type. Prayerfully consider each list and evaluate it in light of what you'd like to see accomplished in the life of your child.

___ *Public School* ___

Advantages:

1. Low cost (if you don't count taxes).

2. Usually close to home.

3. Bus service is often available (although schedules can be a problem).

4. Provides occasional chances to interface with neighbors.

5. Often has good or excellent facilities.

6. Usually offers a wide range of classes and extracurricular activities.

Disadvantages:

1. Often provides a forum for immoral and pagan teaching, and effectively "locks out" God.

2. School environment works against the faith of children, with few kids being able to "witness" against it and most being "witnessed" to by it (see 1 Corinthians 15:33; Ecclesiastes 10:1).

3. Discipline is minimal, nonexistent, or humanistic in orientation.

4. Course work can range from non-Christian to anti-Christian.

5. Government-run, with control of policy coming from many groups other than the parents of the students.

6. Christians can spend vast amounts of valuable time and resources, most of all their children, trying to save something that may not want to be saved.

7. Falling academic standards have become the norm in many school systems.

8. Teaching staffs are judged by things other than merit or excellence.

9. Creates unwanted opportunities for interaction with ungodly children in the neighborhood.

_ *Non-Christian Private School* _

Advantages:

1. Often has good or excellent facilities.

2. Usually offers a wide range of classes and extracurricular activities.

3. Teaching staff tends to be highly educated and skilled.

4. Administration and staff are often very attuned to parents' desires.

5. Diploma can be an excellent credential.

6. Usually has high academic standards.

7. Often has control of students and clear discipline.

8. Children who are disciplinary problems can be expelled.

Disadvantages:

1. As with public schools, God is usually locked out.

2. As with public schools, the environment can work effectively against the faith of children.

3. Discipline can be very humanistic in orientation.

4. Course work can range from non-Christian to anti-Christian.

5. Cost can be extremely high.

6. Schedules and transportation may be inconvenient.

7. Often fosters an elitist mentality in both parents and children.

— Home School —

Advantages:

1. Provides more opportunity for children to know and model themselves after the parent.

2. Can permit additional protection of children from bad influences.

3. Can shield children from peer pressure and allow parents to carefully screen friends.

4. Can help develop friendships within the family.

5. Assuming the parent is truly Spirit-controlled, can provide children with a loving, patient teacher who is concerned for their total well-being.

6. Parents can select and customize curriculum.

7. Provides an opportunity to tie God's truth relevantly into children's lives and academic subjects.
8. Can provide opportunities for parents to pool their efforts and expertise through workshops and other activities.
9. Can be a joy to see children learn and make new discoveries.
10. Can be exciting to learn or relearn along with the children.

Disadvantages:

1. May cater to the self-centered nature of the child and create pride or arrogance.

2. Can easily isolate the family from help within the extended family of God.

3. Passes parental character weaknesses more emphatically along to children.

4. Parents can incorrectly use home schooling as a standard of spirituality, or even as a mark of "super" spirituality.

5. Can enhance the struggle of maintaining authority with the student-child (particularly mothers with their sons), since many more opportunities for conflict and challenge exist.

6. Filling the demanding parent-teacher role creates time challenges, with other domestic areas suffering, initiating potential conflict (especially with an unsupportive spouse).

7. Can be difficult to implement if the weight of the responsibility rests solely on the mother (which it often does).

8. Depending on the training, time, and energy of the parent-teacher, academics can be weak, especially in

later grades (and workshops taught by untrained people may be no better).

___ Christian School ___

Advantages:

1. Can expose children to a variety of godly mentors.

2. Can provide good academic training.

3. Places children in a situation where teachers and parents can have common spiritual goals for them.

4. Can have an atmosphere where God and His Word are honored.

5. Provides children with opportunities for spiritual leadership among their peers.

6. Teachers can provide insights about children where parents have blind spots, especially if parents develop relationships with teachers.

7. Faculty is often very knowledgeable about available Christian curricula and has the training to choose well.

8. Usually every child has the opportunity to participate in any extracurricular activities offered.

9. Disciplinary problems can be dealt with in biblical ways, including expulsion of children who are evil influences (see 1 Corinthians 5:11-13).

10. Often there is significant individual attention and training of children by teachers.

11. Positive peer pressure can often compel even weak children to conform to right behavior.

Disadvantages:

1. Cost can be high.

2. School can be far away and inconvenient to get to.

3. Facilities may be less than excellent.

4. May offer less electives and extracurricular activities than public or non-Christian private schools.

5. May be difficult to achieve a balance between parental and church influence on the school's direction, and between parental and school influence on the child's direction.

6. Children can be "inoculated" to godly living by constant exposure to spiritual exercises, unless they are carefully discipled. Children can learn to parrot right answers and behavior while hiding a hard heart.

7. The administration's goals for the school can sometimes be constrained by financial hardships, which can limit the quality and training of teachers.

8. If it is a church-run school, denominational preferences may be pushed or overemphasized.

9. If it is a parent-run school, spiritual goals and atmosphere can be watered down to the lowest common denominator.

While I couldn't possibly list *every* advantage and disadvantage of a particular school, I hope I've given you a good place to start. And as you evaluate your options, be prepared to ask yourself this question: Am I pleased with the school where my child is spending a fourth of his life?

Education Begins __ with Involvement __

Regardless of the type of school chosen, both parents need to be involved in their children's training in righteousness, if at all possible. All too often, we allow about 50 percent of our parental population to remain largely uninvolved.

Dads, I'm talking about us.

Busy work schedules and other areas of ministry or involvement can drain away most or all of our available time, and we have little or no input to the whole process. Other activities fritter away the last moments that could be used to make a difference. That's just not right.

We dads need to understand more fully how much direction and guidance we can provide for our children. We also need to recognize the reality of the accountability God will hold us to in this important area. He calls us to set the tone for our children's training. Paul beautifully summarizes the father's role in 1 Thessalonians 2:11-12.

Scripture says, "Fathers, do not exasperate your children; *instead*, bring them up in the training and instruction of the Lord" (Ephesians 6:4). A child may be exasperated when his father disciplines him or when he doesn't get his way, but that isn't exasperation—that's fleshly frustration and rebellion. Biblical exasperation occurs when the father isn't doing the primary thing Christian fathers are supposed to do: training and instructing their children.

Two Additional — *Training Topics* —

There are two areas of "training" that may not be part of a formal program, but will be critical to your children's growth. Long after their days in school (of whatever kind) are over, excellence in these two areas will help them to continue to deepen and mature. And these two areas almost *have* to come from within the home. There's little chance that they will be found elsewhere.

These two training topics are the love of reading in general and the use of the Bible in particular.

The Love of Reading

The minds of children are starving for the simple reason that we haven't taught them to read. Now, I am not talking here about the *mechanics* of reading, although we haven't exactly distinguished ourselves in this regard, either. What I am talking about is the *love* of reading, the preference for reading worthy things over the continual nonnutrition of watching television or movies or playing video games.

Mark Twain said: "The man who does not read good books has no advantage over the man who can't read them."

You *must* start reading as a family: you to yourself, so your children can see it isn't torture; you to them, so they can sense your appreciation of good writing and learn how to give the proper sound and sense to the words; they to you, so you can share their interest and determine if they know what they're reading; and they to themselves for wisdom and knowledge.

Teach your kids not only *how* to read, but *what* to read. Some parents think they've done enough when they've gotten their children to read. But they may have done more harm than good. Insist that your children read excellent books and only excellent books. Sixty-six of them are in their Bibles. There are enough other good ones available that they should never have to—or be allowed to—put sewage into their spirits. In the case of bad books, ignorance is indeed a joy and probably also bliss.

Your children will learn from whatever they read, and whatever you allow them to read will, by default, have your stamp of approval on it. Until they reach a deep spiritual maturity that mirrors your own, you should read or at least skim through a book before you allow them to read it. If you haven't read something in a while, reread it with the new insight you've gained as you've grown in the Lord. You'll be amazed that things which used to sound good now sound ungodly and of no value. If you're slow, let your children read the same good books over and over again until you can plow through another one. Be a censor of all that goes into your children's hands and spirits.

Of course, no one can read *everything* that could be useful to their children and still have time to do other things, like walking and breathing. So depend on other godly people in your life to do some of the reading for you. Ask them to make recommendations of books that will enrich your children's lives, extend their knowledge, and enliven their imaginations.

Illiteracy is a creeping destroyer of civilized life. As a person loses words and phrases, he loses the ability to express his ideas, and ultimately the ability to have an original thought. Our children are failing in droves in this very important area. As a parent, you have the responsibility to teach your children to read. You must teach them to read well.

Knowing the Bible

Have you ever noticed how much of your biblical "knowledge" doesn't actually come from the Bible?

We adamantly believe things are in the Bible when the truth is they're not. We are confident that other things are not in the Bible when the plain fact is they are.

God is calling you and me to read, really *read*, the Bible, this wonderful love letter and instruction manual from our heavenly Father. He took the time to spell things out so that we could "find out what pleases the Lord" (Ephesians 5:10).

Reading God's Word with faith and discernment can expose the sin hiding in our hearts, give us wisdom to handle the lousiest of problems, teach us patience to deal with the "thorny" people whom God has stuck in between the roses, and lend us encouragement when nothing in our lives seems to be making any sense.

But we've got to actually read it to get these things. And then we have to teach our children to actually read the Bible, so they can get these things, too. Up until the time they can read for themselves, you must read it to them over and over.

Never let them "not have time" for God's Word. This is where faith will be built up, where wisdom will be stored for future use.

Use any practical device you can find to encourage this personal interest in the Bible itself.

- Set up a poster, a Wisdom Chart, in your kitchen. Let your child put a sticker on for each day that he's read a particular portion of the Bible. A month of stickers is worth an ice cream or dinner out.

- Read some Scripture after one or more of your meals. Have a different person read at least three verses each night. Or, bring an interesting verse or story from the Bible to the table and discuss it.

- Ask your child a question of interest to him. When he asks for the answer (and he will), if he's little, give him the Bible verse; if he's older, give him the chapter or book; if he's 12 or older, give him the concordance.

- Have your child look up things and get back to you with an answer from Scripture.

- Teach your children that bad dreams are most easily disposed of by reading the Psalms. This is infinitely more valuable and effective than tricks like leaving a light on or looking under the bed with them.

- Instruct and encourage these innocent spirits to be young Bereans who look everything up for themselves (see Acts 17:11), no matter who tells them it's in the Bible.

- Here's the toughie: Tell your children that you're really trying to live your life according to your belief in the Bible. Ask them for their help in correcting you if they see an inconsistency between your life and the Bible. You'll be amazed at how much Scripture some of them will start reading!

We deplore the ages when the common man didn't have and couldn't get a Bible for himself. Many people had to rely on secondhand information, tradition, and the authority of the mother church, instead of the actual words of the actual King. But now we have access to dozens of Bibles and hardly use them. Not for life. Not for decisions. Not for obedience. Not for claiming promises. God says repeatedly, in awesome and powerful words, that this wandering from His Word will bring confusion, heartache, and spiritual death.

And if you don't believe me, you can look it up.

13

Training Younger Children

Fiction: Aw, that's okay, he's just a baby. . . .

Fact: Even a child is known by his actions, by whether his conduct is pure and right (Proverbs 20:11).

Even little children can and will be known by the purity and rightness of their conduct. Don't make excuses for the poor behavior of little children. If they're old enough to tell you no, they're old enough to tell you yes!

In this chapter, we'll look at some ideas that apply directly to your younger children.

__ Center of the Universe __

One of the first barriers you'll need to get over with your young children is the idea that they're the center of the universe—that all roads used to lead to Rome, but now they lead to your children.

Parents can compound this so easily by focusing undue attention on their children. We are to seek first the kingdom of God, and no matter how cute they are, your children aren't the whole kingdom of God. They're an important part, but still just a part. Moms, especially, have a tendency to succumb to this. If you see a family where the mom puts *everything* related to her children ahead of almost *everything* else, you know for sure that you're near the center of the universe.

Love isn't rude (1 Corinthians 13:5), but a child at the center of the universe is all too often rude. You don't scream in church and stare at those behind you—and your children shouldn't either. Don't jump every time your children call. Don't give them everything they want. Don't let them whine and complain and generally act like little tyrants. Please don't cause a problem or add to a problem in this area.

When you mix special treatment with the fact that human nature always tends to think it *is* the center of the universe, you can very easily end up with a demanding, egotistical little . . . well, you know.

Nonviolence,
__ *Little Person Style* __

It's absolutely amazing how many adults allow wanton and mindless violence on the part of the young folks, on the unscriptural and nonsensical premise that they're "just kids." Parents tolerate despicable behavior in their children that would cause them to prosecute an adult to the full extent of the law.

Think about it. If most people saw an adult walk up to another adult and hit him on the head with a Tonka truck, they would probably call for the nearest policeman and demand the attacker's arrest. But when little Billy commits mayhem on his peers, what do most people say? "Boys will be boys," or "You can't expect too much from children." They justify it and rationalize it and choose to look the other way.

But what does Scripture say about this?

"Even a child is known by his actions, by whether his conduct is pure and right" (Proverbs 20:11). When your beloved hits or kicks or pinches or pulls on another child, take it for what it is: senseless brutality that shouldn't be tolerated—not even once, not even for a moment.

How do we teach nonviolence? First, set a peaceful example. If you holler and rage, you shouldn't be surprised at your imitative children. Second, restrict a child's intake of violence to as near zero as you can, including contact with violent peers. Kids are just like big people: They do what they see.

Most certainly of all, stop the violence in the hearts of your children. Don't tolerate it in even the smallest measure, and let your kids know how much you abhor it. Discipline it carefully, so they'll know it is a serious crime.

Scripture says we should let our "gentleness be evident to all" (Philippians 4:5) and we should be "completely humble and gentle" (Ephesians 4:2). Scripture makes no exceptions. You shouldn't, either.

When my son Peter was five, he said about his older sister, "The days that we fight—those are the days that aren't fun."

Amen.

A Mouthful of Tongue

Almost everyone has a loose tongue to one extent or another, but nowhere can it be more prevalent, outspoken, and obnoxious than in children. We adults can *think* some gross things about other people, and that's sin enough—but at least we usually don't say aloud everything we think.

The most serious form of tongue abuse is lying. Lying totally devastates the liar as well as its victims. "A lie," said Mark Twain, "can travel half way around the world while the truth is putting on its shoes." God says He hates, He *detests*, a lying tongue (see Proverbs 6:17). If a child lies to cover up a wrong, he should be punished more for the lie than for the wrong—because the lie offends God, because the lie says the child would rather commit another wrong than repent.

The tongue can be used in other offensive ways as well. Children can even outdo adults in using their tongues to exalt themselves. God is clear on this: "If you have played the fool and exalted yourself... clap your hand over your mouth!" (Proverbs 30:32). You should be just as clear.

Keep an eye on a tongue that constantly falls into a pattern of silliness. Plain old foolishness or ungodly sarcasm or cynicism or just a silly flapping tongue can ruin both the flapper and those who listen to him. But do be careful on this one. A sense of humor and the ability to laugh at difficult circumstances can be very valuable in a world that has much to laugh about and much to laugh at.

Another area where you'll probably encounter "tongue problems"? Obscenity. And your children are going to hear more of it than children of earlier generations. Obscenity, especially that which involves the name or person of God, is out of place in Scripture and in the life of His people. You must teach your children to turn their ears away from it and treat it like the unspeakable slime that it is.

Perhaps hurtful comments are the most common examples of children's tongues not under control. God says that "reckless words pierce like a sword" (Proverbs 12:18), and adults, as well as children, can be pierced mortally by the tiniest of reckless people. Don't ignore or humor or tolerate or brush away these comments by saying, "He's only a child." Treat these reckless words as poison and deal with them swiftly and completely.

We have all heard about "wisdom from the mouths of babes." But much more common is lying and complaining and pride and silliness and obscenity and insult and nastiness. God will hold all of us, including our children, accountable for every word we have spoken (see Ecclesiastes 5:2-4; Matthew 12:36-37), and we should expect no less from these little ones. It's our job to teach them how—and when—to speak.

And if they learn, what perfect people they will be (see James 3:2)!

Who's That __ Knocking at My Door? __

By nature, kids aren't courteous beings.

They often can't conceive of anything more important than what's on their minds at any given moment, and they can't imagine why everyone else wouldn't want to hear it—immediately. Their motto is, "He who has an ear to hear, let him hear—loud and clear."

Teach your children to be "quick to listen, slow to speak" (James 1:19).

Start teaching as soon as your children start talking and continue until they stop talking or get married, whichever comes first. Your motto should be: "If they're old enough to talk, they're old enough to keep quiet."

Remind them of a few key proverbs: "He who guards his lips guards his life, but he who speaks rashly will come to ruin"; "A fool's mouth is his undoing, and his lips are a snare to his soul"; "He who guards his mouth and his tongue keeps himself from calamity" (Proverbs 13:3; 18:7; 21:23).

Courtesy in word and interaction should be extended to other people's *privacy* as well. Explain to your children that the reason you have doors is to send them a message: Open doors mean it's all right to come in; closed doors mean knock before entering. Even very little children should be taught to knock on doors—and trained to wait for an answer.

If they do come crashing in, you should invite them right back out and not listen to whatever they have to say. Rudeness seldom has anything to say, nor deserves the right to say it.

And, by the way, you have to return the courtesy. Ask the Lord to help you to respect your children and to command their respect. If you fail, ask the Lord to help you seek their forgiveness of your discourtesy. And then? Go seek your children's forgiveness.

But knock first.

___ *Please Treat Us Alike* ___

"How come I have to do all the work around here? *He* never has to do anything!" "It's not fair I have to go to bed before she does! She's not that much older."

Sooner or later, parents in any family with more than one child are going to hear the call from that bizarre socialistic root that must grow in all of our natural selves: "Please treat us alike."

While children can persuade themselves that all they're asking for is justice, what they really want is more privileges (if the child is younger) or less responsibility (if the child is older).

Jesus has a better idea: "From everyone who has been given much, much will be demanded; and from the one who has been entrusted with much, much more will be asked" (Luke 12:48). The younger child must understand that many responsibilities go along with age and privileges, just as the older child must understand that much of what has been given to him must be taken away if he isn't willing to meet the demands of responsibility.

The way to conquer this problem is to reverse the request of the child. If he's the younger one, offer to give him more responsibility and put all of your emphasis on that (he already thinks he understands the privileges of being older, so you don't need to waste any time on that). If he's the older one, offer to give him fewer privileges and spend all of your discussion time on that (believe me, he *totally* understands the advantages of having less responsibility).

Your objective is to rid them of the jealousy and envy that are bound up in their hearts, and that includes the elimination of this phony demand for "fairness." Pam and I have never had to carry on this kind of conversation for longer than five minutes before the complaining party saw the folly of his statement. Even if your child is a tough case, just implement the plan for a few days and see how he likes it. Don't let him back into his normal role until he cries "uncle."

And he'll think twice—or more—before he says anything the next time.

__ *Losing the Right Things* __

One of the keys to success with children is teaching them to lose the right things.

You might say, "My children are already pretty good at losing things." Children are *experts* at losing things; getting them *not* to lose things would seem to be a higher priority in most homes. But your children are prone to lose things more important than your car keys. They're prone to lose the simplicity that God builds into all of us as He weaves us together in our mothers' wombs.

Children start out in life with childlike faith, trust, love, and simplicity. They also start out in life with a sinful nature and a penchant for evil. They need us to teach them how to keep the first group and lose the second.

Some parents fall for the idea that they have to take a totally blank and faithless spirit and teach it to walk by faith. But they need to understand that their children start out *already* walking by faith. A very little child can't do anything else. He has a simple relationship with God and a simple relationship with you. He *has* to trust others for everything—and he does.

Jesus confirmed this when He said, "I praise you, Father, Lord of heaven and earth, because you have hidden these things from the wise and learned, and revealed them to little children. Yes, Father, *for this was your good pleasure*" (Luke 10:21).

Our goal is to nurture the faith and simplicity that are *already there*. They are delicate and precious possessions. We must be extremely careful to build our children's faith and to grow it into faithfulness. If we allow our children to be exposed to faithless teaching and faithless lives, we shouldn't be surprised to see faith squashed right out of them.

We need to use their simple trust as a weapon to help them eliminate the wrong things from their lives. It's amazing what temptations and sins can creep into the lives of even very little children. But the defense—the shield of faith—is already there, too.

One of the keys to success with children is teaching them to lose the right things.

If we say, "Oh, they're so little. This can't be sin," we abandon our children to the devil's work. If we say, "Oh, I'll just tell my children to stop what they're doing. It'll be all right," we are putting a burden on their backs they're not able to carry. What we need to say is, "This is sin, and I need to teach them how to use their simple faith to resist it."

Then we'll have taught our children to use the right things they have to lose the wrong things they have. And this is victory.

__ *Lights Out!* __

If you've discovered anything of value about evenings, you've probably come to realize the importance of sleep. Staying awake into the wee hours used to be no problem; but now, you're finding yourself dozing on the couch during the eight o'clock television show. For some of us, even comfort isn't required—just being motionless for 30 seconds can do the trick. You also know what happens to you when you don't get enough sleep. You're too tired to spend time with the Lord at night, in the morning, or any other time. You sleep until the last possible minute plus 12, and then rush into the day with your engine wide open. You have to fight back impatience and irritation every step of the way. Nothing seems quite right. Even if it did, it would still make you mad.

Folks, your little children are no different from you, except they haven't figured out the importance of sleep yet.

Now that's a *big* difference. How many parents would have to be argued into going to bed? How many of us would display our creativity by thinking of countless ways to stay awake after our heads have touched the pillow? Most of us *enjoy* sleeping. But here arc these children, and they hate the whole idea. To be blunt, they think the idea of going to bed stinks. It looks like a waste of time to them; besides, they're sure they'll miss something.

But sleep isn't a waste of time, and you *want* them to miss something. They need it for themselves, so they can be physically refreshed. They can't be strong in Christ if they're fighting a body that's out of control. And you can't parent properly if your children are up until you don't have the time and energy to do anything else but collapse into a chair. It's an amazing relationship: *Their* sleep will bring *you* rest. You'll be able to commune with God and with your spouse, and figure out exactly what it was you did that day. You want your children to miss this regrouping time. If they don't, you won't have one.

Create a fixed and fairly inflexible "lights out" time, rather than a set bedtime. Allow 30 minutes, even for ones as little as two or three years old, to listen to tapes or read books after they've gotten into bed. If they know the lights are going out at 8:30, come what may, they'll have an incentive to get into bed by eight to maximize their time. If they get into bed at 8:15 because of their own lack of discipline and focus, they still have lights out at 8:30 and their time is cut to 15 minutes.

It's important for you to insist that they do their "noodling" on their own time. Going to the bathroom, getting a drink, finding their lost poopsie bear, giving you a hug, and so on—all of this must happen in their 30 minutes or before. And don't battle the evening clean-up, either. Let them know what you expect and where things should go. Let them know that anything not put away will be picked up by you and put in *your* closet, for a week or two.

Start dinner and the evening early enough so that the family as a whole and the children in particular have time to spend quietly and joyfully together. And plan your evening so that you'll have at least two hours after "lights out" before you go to sleep.

Finally, if you're reading this in the evening, and you're finding yourself slipping away, I've only got one more thing to say: Lights out.

14

Training Older Children

Fiction: Just wait till you have teenagers!

Fact: Your sons and daughters will prophesy, your young men will see visions (Acts 2:17).

We want to raise children who, as young men and women, will prophesy—speak forth—the Word of God into a dying culture. We want young people who will see visions of what can be accomplished in their day for the kingdom of God.

In this chapter, we'll explore some ideas that I hope will help.

___ *I'm in Love with Me* ___

Many young men and women are legends in their own minds.

A fine-sounding but terribly destructive idea circulating these days says that children must have a well-developed sense of self-esteem if they're to be successful. We're also told that low self-esteem can have tremendous destructive power in children's lives. Parents can be gullible, so we encourage our children to take pride in themselves and be self-confident. We encourage them, basically, to fall in love with themselves. And then we are amazed when they actually *do* these things and become "independent"—or even egotistical and arrogant.

If you listen to most psychiatrists or psychologists, you get the idea that the lack of self-esteem is a serious problem facing all of us, especially young people. In a way, this is true. You don't have to look into the eyes of an abandoned or abused child for very long to see that he doesn't like himself very much. There's an even larger group of young people who stay with their parents until adulthood, but whose unloved hearts end up in the same shattered place.

The world, of course, has a solution to this problem: Encourage your child to take pride in himself; as a result, your child will have enough confidence to live his own life in his own way. The problem is, this just substitutes one sin for another. Instead of committing the sin of hating God's creation (themselves), your children are encouraged in the sin of pride. It's true that the world has too much sadness and tears and loneliness; it's equally true that the world has too much pride and self-centeredness. Way too much.

In the choice of the lesser of these two evils, we as parents should choose neither.

---

*You need to teach your children that they
have immense and special value as beings
created in the image and likeness
of a perfect and holy God.*

Our real problem is that we don't understand the value of low self-esteem. You don't have to look very far in Scripture to find that God, in fact, is in the business of *causing* low self-esteem. "The LORD tears down the proud man's house" (Proverbs 15:25).

God's desire is to bring all men to Him. The greatest obstacle to this is high self-esteem; therefore, "God opposes the proud" (James 4:6). He warns us not to think higher thoughts about ourselves than we ought (see

Romans 12:3). Our lives lived in the flesh shouldn't justify very high thoughts about ourselves anyway.

You need to teach your children that they have immense and special value as beings created in the image and likeness of a perfect and holy God. They should know that the *only* thing of eternal value in the physical universe is people. They should be told that they were so loved, in fact, that God Himself became a man to pour out His life so they might live. They should be constantly reminded that an infinitely filled God emptied Himself so they might be filled to overflowing.

But they also need to know that this connection with perfection was lost through the sin of pride—the very same thing that's being sold as the "solution" to our problems. But pride is not the solution to the problem of low self-esteem. Pride is, in fact, the problem that *causes* low self-esteem.

Scripture is plain: "Let him who boasts boast in the Lord" (1 Corinthians 1:31; 2 Corinthians 10:17). Pride leads away from God, which eventually produces an even lower self-esteem. Pride broke our connection with God in the first place, and the substitution of pride for low self-esteem only makes the break wider. Let your child take pride, but let him take it in *God*.

Your children must be taught to believe that they can't spend the rest of their lives feeling good about themselves by their own efforts. Tell them that if they do, the doubts will come and they'll fall to even lower self-esteem. They must become convinced in their own hearts that being proud of God and others (see 2 Corinthians 7:4; Philippians 2:3) is the only truly satisfying kind of esteem.

Your children need *God*-confidence, not self-confidence. Give this to them from the ground up. Children trained from infancy to devote their lives to high God-esteem won't have to deal with inferiority rubbish, because their minds are on God and the kingdom and not on themselves.

Teach your children to love God, not themselves. There's a lot more there to love.

___ *The Birds and the Bees* ___

Many of us were raised to think that dating the opposite sex is just as natural as going to church on Sunday mornings. Dating has been so acceptable for so long that we have convinced ourselves it is part of a Christian's life. We are fairly sure we could even muster some Scripture to dating's defense.

Stop reading right now, go to the Word, and find every passage that justifies and supports the custom of dating.

That didn't take long, did it? The whole scheme of dating that's been constructed in this culture simply doesn't have anything to do with God's best for our children. There's not a shred of biblical evidence to support dating.

So how are my kids supposed to meet the right person? you might be thinking. *Certainly you're not proposing arranged marriages . . . are you?*

You've found me out—but before you fall out of your chair, listen for a moment.

Everything good or of value in a Christian's life is arranged by God. *Everything.* "Then I said, 'Here I am, I have come—it is written about me in the scroll' " (Psalm 40:7). "LORD, you have assigned me my portion and my cup" (Psalm 16:5). Scripture asks, "A wife of noble character who can find?" (Proverbs 31:10). And Scripture answers: "A prudent wife is from the LORD" (Proverbs 19:14).

So, a young person—or for that matter, an older person—has a mate picked out for him by God, if he is to be married. Did you hear that? Picked out by *God.*

Now ask yourself: Is a person going to find his (or her) God-picked partner by a random plowing through the masses that make up the opposite sex? Or is God more likely to give him leading and guidance through a God-ordained authority—like his own parents?

You might be thinking that *any* person whom your child marries is "of the Lord"; otherwise, God wouldn't have "allowed" it to happen. But that thinking says that actions don't have consequences, that Christians can't make mistakes or miss God's leading, and that whatever a Christian might do is good because God wouldn't have let it happen otherwise. That's not scriptural.

If you are lawfully married and "found" your partner by dating, I'm not proposing that you begin a new search for your self using better methods. God no longer has any options for you except to remain married and to let Him make it the best it can be. Maybe your marriage turned out great in spite of dating. Good! But does that mean we can't do better, raise our standards even higher, develop a sense of dignity and respect even further?

Give your children the vision that a godly life, and godly relationships, are more important than dating. By your own relationships with adults of the opposite sex, help your kids to see how they can have deep, rich, intimate, holy, and pure relationships with young people of the opposite sex. And encourage your children to consider singleness as a blessing rather than a curse. God starts everyone out single, so it must not be too bad an option.

There will be, of course, times for your children to relate to other young people. So set some ground rules. Generally, limit their contact to other growing Christians. Make sure activities are done in larger groups (no one-on-one). Try to have the event at your house. And make sure chaperons will be present.

If you have a daughter, how should she handle requests for dates? Have your daughter tell him no. If he wants more details or just won't go away, she should tell him to talk with her dad. That will probably end the discussion. If he has the courage to call you, Dad, use it as an opportunity to teach the young man about (no) dating, and about friendship and courtship. And what do you do if God's "gift" to your child seems to be in view? The way is simple. The entire subject should be laid at God's feet. You and your child should be in prayer, the Word, and discussion together. Times to relate to a potential partner should be set up within the context of families, so that you, your child, the potential partner, and his or her parents have the same basis for discernment. You'll go through the relationship *together*. Ideally, there will be no disagreement between you and your child before a marriage is planned. Rather, you should arrive at the absolute certainty that this person is, indeed, the one.

Discerning the person whom God has picked, in other words, is a family project. It isn't arranged by the parents alone, using only cultural traditions. Marriage is arranged by God, and two whole families and churches get to be involved in the process.

And while your children are single, give them a vision for staying home. Let them know that they don't have to move out to be an "adult" and have their own home. Your children already *have* a home. Learn to adjust your thinking about your children over the years so that by the time they're adults living in your home, you're *treating* them like adults living in your home.

And may every one of your children joyously and comfortably stay with you, until God makes it joyously and comfortably clear that marriage is His plan.

___ *Peers* ___

A lot of people spend their time looking for ways to find some decent peers for their children. Youth groups, Bible clubs, summer camps—the ways are endless. In some churches, peer-group activity has become almost an entertainment business.

What draws kids to the youth group at your church? If it's the Lord, then you've got something special and you ought to treasure it. But if it's the activities, the music, the food, the chance to get away from adults, the chance to goof off with other kids, then you are probably not accomplishing much of anything positive—and you might even be doing harm.

Your kids don't need to be entertained. They don't need to spend gobs of time with other kids their own age, either. In real life, people have to relate to people of many different ages. *You* have to relate to people of many different ages. Get your children in on the real world.

Peers can be an overwhelming force in the life of an older child. If your children aren't peer dependent, and they lean toward you and other authority, congratulate their wisdom by letting them make as many of their own decisions as possible. If they *are* peer dependent, make sure your kids know that the price they must pay for this is a loss of decision-making power. Decision-making requires wisdom, and peer-dependence is not wise.

All that glitters isn't gold. Peers and peer groups can glitter.

But they aren't gold.

___ *What I Did for Christ* ___

A number of years ago, there was a popular song on Broadway, "What I Did for Love." In the play, some of the characters were complaining that their careers hadn't been as "rewarding" as they had hoped. The singer rebuked them for even thinking such a thing; she had chosen her career for love of the profession and hadn't expected anything else. In a time when people are choosing careers to avoid being under authority or to

grab as many material things as possible, it is a refresh-
ing song (even though the play itself has some real
problems).

The sad truth is that relatively few people today do
anything career-related for reasons other than the love of
self and the love of money. The basic question is: What
pleases me? More often than not, the underlying reasons
for starting a business are: 1) "I want to be my own boss"
(rebellion); and 2) "I want to keep more money for myself"
(greed). These aren't the kinds of reasons that appeal to
God.

I was discouraged from pursuing a desired career
path because, "There's no money in that," and "You'll
never go anywhere in that field." My only argument was
that it was the direction of my heart, in spite of the
obvious problems. But it wasn't enough to stem the tide
of practical arguments against it.

Those arguments were wrong. I've heard other parents and counselors give the same misdirected advice.
Too many people, if *they* can't see obvious and immediately bountiful payback, try to steer others from going
the way God Himself might be encouraging.

We who are in the household of God need to set our
criteria much higher than position or money or even
love. We should create an environment for our children
where they can make their choices based on doing their
life's work for *Christ*, and for no other reason. Only what
they do for Christ will satisfy them.

Your child will spend a huge portion of the rest of his
life in his career. Be in prayer. You want it to count for
God to the maximum.

Encourage your kids not to do *anything* for money.
What they need will be added to them if they seek God's
path for them first and only (see Luke 12:31). Aside from
this glorious promise, they would be much better off
living in a tent and doing what Christ wants them to do,
than living in a mansion and hating every minute of

their labor. God *wants* them to enjoy and be satisfied with their work (see Ecclesiastes 2:24; 3:12-13; 3:22; 5:18-20; 8:15).

Spend enough time with your child to learn about his deepest motivations and desires—as they relate to serving Christ and others, not *himself*. Sentences that begin with "I want" or "I need" or "I'd like to" should be looked at closely. God isn't interested in satisfying selfish desires. He knows that the only way for this child's deepest wants and needs and likes to be satisfied is for him to give them up to his Lord and yield his life to others.

I suggest that you keep a piece of paper called "career paths" somewhere where it will come to your attention often—in your Bible, taped to the front of your television, or in the drawer with the Milk Duds. Have a list of the current possibilities for each of your children written down, with a note or two on why this is a possibility and how it can be explored or developed. This would be a perfect thing to bring up regularly when you're together on an outing.

As you develop this list, don't assume your child should do what you're doing, or what you've always dreamed he should do. But at the same time, you shouldn't assume a passive role in this process. God doesn't want you to dictate his career, but He does expect you to lead and guide and influence the process. Have a powerful influence in this area of your child's life. He knows more about his heart's desires, but you know more about life.

Make sure you include on your daughter's list the *possibility* of being a full-time wife and mother. That may not be God's choice for her, but if it is, He wants her to be a wife and mother in an excellent way.

Unless your children are absolutely sure of their chosen path, I strongly suggest you consider having them take a break of one to two years after high school, to take

some time to think and to plan. Together, you can strate-
gize ways to accomplish things that could not have been
done earlier. When they do go on to college or some
other career path, they will be much more mature, knowledgeable, and experienced.

One final reminder is in order. Encourage your children to remember that their primary business on earth
isn't to pursue a career, even a God-inspired one. Their
primary business is to pursue *God*. So the song, at last, is
true: What they do should be for love.

Of God.

Epilogue

We have covered a lot of ground in this book. But I want to close with a simple thought, a little reminder from a fellow pilgrim:

You can do it.

May God bless you richly in your efforts as you follow Him.

And may *every one* of your children shine like a star in the universe (Philippians 2:15).

Acknowledgments

I gratefully acknowledge the wonderful efforts of the team at Harvest House—particularly the insight and direction of Eileen Mason, and the excellent editorial work and special encouragement of Barbara Sherrill. I would also like to give special thanks to Bridgett O'Lannerghty, who contributed to the editorial process and stood with me throughout the project. I deeply appreciate the input and support of Diane, a long-time friend, and many others who contributed their prayers, input, and love.

I also want to give a deep thanks to two women who affected the direction of my life in a special way—Anna LaVerne, my mom, who was the first to say, "Marry Pam"; and Nancy Lee, my spiritual mother, who helped introduce me to Christ and allowed me to marry her one and only daughter.

Finally, I want to thank those listed on the dedication page for their "dedication" to me: Pam, who has believed in this work, and labored with me through every inch of it and the parenting itself; Laura, Peter, David, and Bethany, who have been more than understanding of the time it takes to write, and have been gracious recipients of our attempts at applying these principles; and Maryl, who has supported this effort in every way, and supplied many of the good questions and examples that fed into this book. This family is more than I ever had a right to ask for or imagine.

About the Author

James R. Lucas has been involved with the training of children within the church for two decades. He has served as a pastor, youth pastor, and Sunday school superintendent, and is deeply interested in improving this process and centering it firmly within the family unit. He has also been a management executive with several different companies, and the president of Luman Consultants, a management consulting firm.

Mr. Lucas is the author of the Christian novels, *Weeping in Ramah* (Crossway Books) and *Noah: Voyage to a New Earth* (Wolgemuth & Hyatt). He lives with his wife and four children in the Kansas City area.

Mr. Lucas welcomes your comments and requests for additional information. Please write him at:

James R. Lucas
P.O. Box 2566
Shawnee Mission, KS 66201